PORTRAITS OF THE TEDWORTH FOX

Richard Burton, Huntsman to Thomas Assheton Smith Esq., with hounds at Tedworth House 1841.
Print by kind permission of Mrs. Michael Burke-Gaffney.

PORTRAITS OF THE TEDWORTH FOX

Estelle Holloway

With best wishes

Estelle

By the same author

"Elinor with the Pleading Eyes".

"Hounds, Hares and Foxes of Larkhill"
The Story of the Royal Artillery Hunt.
Both books obtainable from
Mrs. Holloway, Oriel House,
Bolland's Hill, Seend, Melksham SN12 6NQ.

ISBN 0 9512104 1 6

A CIP catalogue record for this book is obtainable from the British Library.
Printed and Typeset by the West Somerset Free Press,
5 Long Street, Williton, Taunton, Somerset TA4 4QN
Published by the author

Obtainable from either the author or
all good booksellers especially
Messrs. J. A. Allen & Co, The Huntsman's Bookshop Ltd,
1 Lower Grosvenor Place,
Buckingham Palace Road, London SW1 W0EL

DISCLAIMER
Every possible effort has been made to contact copyright holders of photographs reproduced in this work.
The author can entertain no claim from any person after publication.

PORTRAITS OF THE TEDWORTH FOX

The Story of the Tedworth Hunt

by
Estelle Holloway

The author would like to thank:

The Hunt Committee, Master and Hunt Staff for their help and co-operation towards this project. In particular, John Wallis Esq, for his information, patience and suggestions in reading the script.

Former Masters and others who have hunted with the pack, for interviews, letters and diaries giving reminiscences and amusing anecdotes, especially to J. M. Read Esq for his interesting tape-recording. Also to the Honourable Mrs. Mirabel Helme.

The Hunt Secretary Miss Rhonda Small for her encouragement, and for 'putting me right' on many, many occasions; and Mr. and Mrs. Wheeler for correcting assorted spelling mistakes!

Lady Dulverton for her memories of Sir Peter Farquhar and Lord Melchett.

And, of course, the many persons mentioned in the text and in the reference section who have contributed to "Portraits of the Tedworth Fox."

Very special thanks are given to Captain B.E. Fanshawe, who has found time from the exigency of the "B.F.S.S. Campaign for Hunting", to contribute such an interesting and amusing Foreword.

Sketches of local scenes are by Nicholas Barry-Tait.

List of Pre-Publication Subscribers to this book

Michael Ancram M.P.
Margot Andrews
Mr. and Mrs. John Bamber
Wendy Barnes
Mr. and Mrs. J. S. Barry-Tait
Geraldine Beaton
Nigel Beckhowgh
Josephine Burnfield
Flight Lieutenant and Mrs. Tim Burgess
Colonel and Mrs. P. R. R. de Burgh
Mr. and Mrs. J. Burrett
Dr. C. B. Cameron
David Campion C.R.E., T.D.
Mrs. Charles Cardiff
Captain Baron Jacques de Cartier d'Yves
Miss Catherine Channon
Jenny Clarke
Major W. G. Clarke
Carol Cole
Nigel Cousins
T. M. Curtis
Major W. G. Crosbie Dawson
Charles and Dinah Dickson
Mr. and Mrs. H. F. W. Donauer
Isabel Drewry
Ruth, Lady Dulverton
Malcolm and Janet Firth
Richard J. C. Ford
Alma J. Fowle
Alex Gay
Mr. and Mrs. C. H. B. Gibson
Mrs. Audrey Goodwin
Colonel and Mrs. Nick Gow
Judy Grange
Pamela Griffiths and Robin Stanbridge
The Hon. Erskine Guinness
The Hon. F. B. Guinness
D. B. Hammerson
Hampsley Hollow Riding Centre
Sam Hart R.N. (retd)
Terence M. Harvey
Mr and Mrs P. Hayes
Lieutenant Colonel P. R. Heaton-Ellis
Lesley Heavens and Alan Dale
The Hon. Mirabel Helme
Mr. and Mrs. E. Hill
Mr. and Mrs. N. J. Hills
Mr. and Mrs. Philip Hodson
Mr. and Mrs. Michael Holliday
Michael Holloway
Gavin R. M. Hudson
Jonathan Inglesant T.D., J.P., M.R.A.C.
Captain and Mrs. R. J. Inglesant M.F.H.
Lieutenant Colonel John Jago
S. K. Kirk
Christopher Lee
Lieutenant Colonel and Mrs. J. N. Leonard
Val Lynch
Barbara MacMullen
Clare Macnamara
Lieutenant Colonel and Mrs. L. W. McNaught
Rita McVittie
Brian Marlow
Mrs. Julia Mason
Sir Charles Morrison
Keith M. Morrison
Elizabeth, Lady Moyne
Charlotte Munby
Jennifer Munby
John Nicholas
Michael Nicholas
Peter Nicholas
Major G. H. W. Oakford
Rachelle Ormond
Brigadier Peter Painter
Kate Powell
Mrs. D. E. Rawlins
Bryan J. L. Read
James C. Read
J. M. Read
Samuel Read
John Reynolds
J. W. Ritchie
Major Jimmy Robertson
Major James Scott
Mrs. M. R. Sampson
Mrs. R. Scrimgeour
Brian Sedgley
Miss Rhonda Small
John and Carol Snook
Mr. and Mrs. A. G. Sims
Charles Spencer
Chris Morgan-Smith
Captain and Mrs. G. H. Stanning R.N. (retd)
Lieutenant Colonel K. A. P. Stevenson
J. N. Swanson
Mrs. J. M. Swanwick
Major and Mrs. G. D. B. Thatcher
Brian Toogood
Ian Vowell
John and Di Wallis
Hilary Wheeler
Roger Wheeler
Lieutenant Colonel J. F. Willcocks

FOREWORD
BY BRIAN FANSHAWE

How lucky we are to have such people as Estelle Holloway to write so feelingly about their local communities, the hounds and the hunting, the characters and the countryside as a whole. We should all write and read much more. How I now regret not keeping my hunting diaries more assiduously.

In retrospect, not finding the time was a poor excuse. However, finding time, energy and horses to hunt elsewhere when one is hunting a pack of hounds oneself is difficult.

For various personal reasons the Tedworth is somewhere I should have tried to pinch a day. So it was a great pleasure to make direct contact with the Tedworth in the summer of 1994 when I was asked to judge their Puppy Show. The young Master, Rupert Inglesant, and his wife Caroline produced enough food and drink to replete most of Tidworth Garrison for a week, as well as exhibiting a remarkably level and fit young entry.

Rupert is the first of three examples to illustrate the small world of foxhunting. He was brought up in Leicestershire where his father was a very popular and effective secretary to the Quorn for a number of years. Both father and son were the most knowledgeable and energetic foot followers of the Quorn, Cottesmore and Fernie—with Rupert appearing mounted whenever he could beg, borrow or steal a horse—it paid to hold onto your reins if you had a fall on a day when Inglesant Jnr. was running. The founder of the Tedworth in 1826 was Thomas Assheton Smith, previously he was the Master of the Quorn in the days when they also hunted the present Fernie country.

At the Puppy Show I found Peter Horton, now farming in Exmoor but for 14 seasons the Tedworth's most successful post-war Master and Huntsman. In 1967 I bought one of the best huntsman's horses I have ever ridden from Peter. She was rather a plain mare and she failed the vet; however, I don't recall whether it was Peter's whisky, my dearth of horse-power at the time or just a whim I had about the mare. I bought her regardless. I hunted hounds off her for five seasons in Warwickshire and Galway before selling her for a large profit to my joint Master—no vet! She didn't so much have a fifth leg, she might be described as a centipede.

Also at the Puppy Show was my mother, now well into her eighties and living at Milton Lilbourne, a mile or two from the present kennels. Her eye and interest in hounds remain undimmed—"What was wrong with that big dark hound?" was her first question to me when we finished our judging. Her Tedworth connections go back to the late 1920s when her brother, Sir Peter Farquhar, first made his mark as a huntsman with the Tedworth hounds. My father whipped in before he too hunted the Tedworth for a season—they were both serving officers at Tidworth and queued up to be orderly officer on Sundays. There are two treasures that remain in my family—a silver hunting horn presented to my parents from the Tedworth Farmers on the occasion of their marriage in 1932 and a female line to Sophie 27 bought in by my Uncle Peter. That line has been retained ever since by Farquhars or Fanshawes particularly by my mother during the war and recently returned from me to Ian Farquhar at Badminton.

Perhaps one day I will appear on Salisbury Plain with a silver hunting horn and a bitch or two from the family line—Rupert, sit tight!

Chapter 1

Tedworth House 1833.

Throw Your Heart Over . . . . . .

"Throw your heart over. And your horse will follow" was a favourite expression of Mr. Thomas Assheton Smith. A brilliant horseman and one of the most prominent huntsmen of the day, he founded the Tedworth Hunt in 1826.

Mr. Smith did not become a master of foxhounds because it was the fashion to be a master. Neither did he ride up close to his hounds one day, only to loiter a mile behind them the next. He was always the same man. The same desperate fellow over a country, and he had the most bulldog-like nerve in the saddle.

At the time Tom Smith knew he could soon inherit Tedworth House and estate from his aged father, no other hunt was interested in the desolate chalk uplands of Salisbury Plain, or its cramped river valleys. Therefore it was towards the Craven country lying in the east that he looked to found his own pack of foxhounds. Except for the month of March, when the elephantine John Warde, described by Nimrod as the "father of foxhunting" brought his Craven pack to Weyhill, little sport was possible. Chute forests, including Faccombe Copse, Doles and Harewood made an impenetrable crescent surrounding Andover and Weyhill, while Ashdown* Copse, probably planted by a Smith ancestor, had grown to unmanageable proportions.

Landowners laughed when Smith proposed to pursue the fox from Weyhill.

"It is all flint," they said. "Flints and forest."

Smith opened up several hundred square miles to create a completely new hunting country, and laid the foundation of a pack which has hunted with pride for nearly 170 years.

The major portion of the country lies in Wiltshire and includes the Salisbury Plain area, Pewsey Vale and Savernake Forest. A map published by J & C Walker after 1841, when the Great Western Railway was the first of a network of railroads to mesh Wiltshire with Hampshire shows a series of dots depicting 'places of the meeting of foxhounds'. Modern maps are

**Originally known as Ashley Coppice the name may be a corruption of Assheton.*

not so accommodating. Mr. T. A. Smith's country, now the Tedworth, lies as far as the medieval coachroad linking Salisbury with Foxley Corner, near Devizes, as its western boundary with the South and West Wilts. To the north-west is the Duke of Beaufort's prestigious hunt, while north of Marlborough the Vale of the White Horse pack adjoins Craven country. The New Forest hunt lies to the south.

Thomas Assheton Smith's biographer was Sir John Eardley-Wilmot, and the book was an attempt to rescue Smith's character from virulent aspersions written in one of the journals. Such a charismatic person attracted enemies, and newspaper articles were even more scandalous than they are today, in their efforts to sell hot gossip. However if his hero possessed one quarter of the manly qualities ascribed to him, Tom must have been a very great fox-hunting gentleman indeed! Immensely wealthy and hard-riding he certainly was, but with light hands holding silken reins, being adored by horse and hound alike.

Reminiscences of the late Thomas Assheton Smith Esq. was printed in 1860 by John Murray of Albemarle Street, London. Bound in fox-red cloth, a fearsome fox's mask with crossed brushes, and crossed hunting whips, all in gold, decorates the cover. Primrose yellow paper adorns the reverse front and back bindings, and the original reader had to cut the handmade paper with his paper-knife to separate the pages.

Opening the book, the frontispiece depicts Assheton Smith astride his horse and is a copy of a painting by Cooper. The eyes beneath heavy brows are large, composed and strangely penetrating. The oval face and classical features may have been the fashionable genre of the artist. However, the picture implies a powerful, intelligent man, and unlike the clothes conscious peacocks of Regency days, the cut of his jacket shows him as a plain fellow. They said he made a greatcoat last twelve years.

Rich and talented, the power-house of his fortune came from ship-building and slate quarries inherited from his mother Elizabeth, the daughter of Watkin Wynn of Voelas, north Wales.

Born 7 August 1776 and known as plain Tom Smith he learned the rudiments of hunting when a boy with some rabbit beagles on Sedbury (Sidbury) Hill, less than three miles from Tedworth House. Heavily wooded and flanked by prehistoric earthworks, this early British fortress still harbours deer, hare, fox and game birds. Home from Eton for the holidays, Tom hunted his father's distinguished pack of foxhounds showing excellent sport. His father appears to have been both proud and jealous of Tom's horsemanship, while "Scrutator" alias Mr. Horlock of the Craven speaks in glowing terms of this brilliant pack. The *Foxhound Kennel Studbook* which was started in 1841 (1800-1844) shows that in 1824 Trimbush was sired by the eleven year old Brocklesby Trimbush by Mr. Warde's Candid, while in 1826 Clasher was by Belvoir Rallywood out of Tedworth Chantress. The first edition of the F.K.S.B. was compiled by Mr. Vyner ("Notitia Venatica") and Mr. Cornelius Tongue ("Cecil") in 1866. The preface to the reprinted edition in 1906 says that hounds entered are only those in each year's entry which were ultimely bred from.

In 1794 Tom went up to Christ Church, Oxford, as a gentleman commoner. He hunted regularly in Oxfordshire and Northamptonshire. He rowed and played cricket, to become one of England's best bats as a member of Mr. Lord's Marylebone Cricket Club. But cricket was only a summer diversity. From October to March he dedicated himself to the chase.

From 1800 while hunting in Leicestershire, Assheton Smith's sportsmanship became a legend in the country, until in 1806 he made his debut as master of foxhounds by following Lord Foley as Master of the Quorn. For nine seasons until 1816, Smith resided at Quorndon Hall with fine horses and splendid hounds, many of them bought for a thousand guineas from his friend Jack Musters. Such an establishment had to be paid for. It is said Tom's father had to sell his Sutton estate, near Winchester racecourse, to finance the Quorn mastership.

A desperate horseman, "I'll be with my hounds" was Tom's motto. Unless left behind by a fall, and he had heart-breaking falls, he never took his eye off the pack, while nothing stopped him during casts. With his coarse language and zeal to show sport, his horses Jack O'Lantern, Tom Thumb or the Big Grey carried this bulldog of a man over ugly bullfinches and impossible ditches because as a huntsman he knew how many foxes are lost by stopping at a fence during the crucial moments.

A headstrong, stubborn fellow with a violent temper, Tom loved a fight. In the 1818 election, he contested the Liberal stronghold of Nottingham for the Tories. And the town was placarded with:

"No foxhunting M.P.!"

Times do not change much. When he tried to speak at the hustings, electors burnt a guy dressed in a red coat with a fox's brush dangling from its behind. Perhaps it was also part of a "smear campaign" when *The Field* thundered:

"Mr. Smith takes refuge in Middleton's Bank!"

According to Eardley-Wilmot's defence Tom had hitched his horse's bridle over the iron railings of the bank. Unfortunately the animal stood across the street to the chagrin of a coaldrover, who might have been a Liberal. He struck the horse with his whip, nearly sending him through the bank's window. Tom rushed out steaming with rage, and being a proficient boxer there was a grand punch-up until the police arrived with drawn truncheons.

Later Tom sent the drover five pounds as compensation, although enemies said he paid the man, who was known as the local prize-fighter, to go away.

After giving up Leicestershire where Mr. Osbaldeston succeeded him at the Quorn, Smith took his stud to Lincoln to work the Burton country. Until 1824 fame and fortune were his. Many of the Melton men followed him knowing they were sure of superexcellent sport. However, dykes such as the "Tilla" were formidable, and Meltonians soon tired of floundering in bottomless slime. By 1826, perhaps at sick parents' request, Tom decided to return home, and live at Penton Lodge, near Weyhill, close to the Hampshire/Wiltshire border.

While at Penton, his quick eye noted the vacancy between the New

Forest and Craven hunt boundaries. Since boyhood he had longed for a country of his own. Except for John Warde's month at Weyhill, no hound had ever opened in those big chases. And during the first year Tom started to hunt this wilderness of tree and flint with a scratch pack. Owing to the scarcity of foxes and the wildness of the pack, only four and a half brace were accounted for during the season. So in 1827, according to Nimrod, he hunted Sir Richard Sutton's famous hounds. But Penton Lodge stables were small, therefore, new stabling, together with kennels had to be built in great haste.

Today walking behind Penton Lodge the back of an impressive E-shaped block of brick stables and coach-house designed by Smith line the roadway. Kennels, it is said, lay on the other side of the road. Dick Burton, following from the Quorn, must have led the splendid new hounds between brick gate-pillars, and then left-handed past a windbelt of holly, oak and box to the courtyard. Here the racket of carpenters' hammers greeted the pack, as workmen completed the construction of the two-storied wings of the "E" design. The 120 foot long middle section is crowned by a central clock-tower, ornate and dark grey with age. Its elegant pointed steeple being surmounted by a high weathercock, depicting a strong fox leaping across swordlike grass. Clock hands have stopped at five to eleven as though in sadness, because time remembers that "They Meet at Eleven". Standing on the road to peer through barred windows of the coach-house, one can see the shoulders of a statue of the Blessed Virgin as this has become a school chapel. Ivy-clad walls lean outwards in decline.

Penton Lodge is an unexceptional Georgian house. In cold October light, and fringed by groups of dreary box-bushes, it shines pale grey, to give a wraithlike appearance. However, the long windows of this plain, small demesne, must have blazed with candlelight on the evening of the 29 October 1827, that Mr. Smith brought his bride Matilda, the second daughter of William Webber of Binfield Lodge, Berkshire, to their Hampshire home. Then a man of fifty-one, he would have entertained the wedding-guests wearing a red coat with white facings, his elegant legs — he was proud of his legs — encased in white silk stockings.

These were the days of rapturous buoyancy,[1] reflected in bridal costumes. Perhaps Matilda, being a quiet lady, wore a gown of India muslin, although the neckline was excessively décolleté, with a profusion of beads and braids, bands and bows. A bride's hair was tied in an Apollo knot, to contrast with the enormous evening hats of other ladies. Hats which were loaded with silk or satin trimmings of ridiculous size.

But Mr. Smith was a plain man in the mornings, when dawn meant hunting as usual, even after a wedding night with a new bride. Five foot ten inches in height he weighed eleven and a half stone and his appetite was prodigious. Breakfast was the main meal of his day, and comprised one dish, mutton hash. Cooks might yawn at the four o'clock hour before cub-hunting, but it was easy to drag great pans of mutton and onion topped with potato, from the oven of a wood-burning stove. Mutton that had braised all night to greet the Master in the hall. Here he stood gulping down plateful after plateful, as he discussed with his whippers-in a plan for the morning.

This was the important last meet before the season opened in November.

A month later in December 1827, Nimrod visited Mr. and Mrs. Tom Smith at Penton. There was no honeymoon for Matilda. Hunting came first. Nimrod speaking of the country said:

"There is nothing but beds of flints. And as for Hampshire woodlands they are the worst in the known world. When I first heard of his hunting the Andover country, I thought it a mere frolic of the day."

That was the month of the great meet at Weyhill, with the Master mounted on Rob Roy, and George Gardener as first whipper-in. Three hundred of the landed gentry rode to the first draw to view the magnificent pack. There were smiles and whispers behind hands, because they knew hunting was impossible due to the badness of scent, and the country had not been preserved long enough to ensure a find. Nimrod takes up the story:

"Scent was wretchedly bad, but hounds stooped to it like rabbit beagles. Anyone would have had a treat in seeing this highly bred pack pick their way, inch by inch over a stubble field. Mr. Smith, whose patience and judgment were conspicuous on this trying occasion, had the eyes of a very large field upon him. But he never lifted his hounds a yard, though the line of country was apparently before him. And thus did he hit off his fox, for the fox did not take that line."

A further comment by Nimrod says:

"He was particularly careful in making his casts, often three in number each one wider than the other and spreading like a skyrocket"

Sporting Magazine March 1840

Later he added Sir Thomas Burghey's hounds to his pack.

In spite of Tom always accounting for his fox, and extraordinary though it may appear, his father hated the idea of him turning his back on the fat grass countries of Leicestershire to hunt Hampshire's dense woodlands. To the old man the idea was ridiculous. Thus the father being as stubborn as his son, he was the only landowner to refuse Tom permission to hunt his copses.

"And where does young Tom think he is going to meet next week?" he asked a neighbour.

"Ashdown Copse. So 'tis said."

"Ashdown Copse!" stormed the old man. "If he does. The puppy. I'll bring an action on him. For trespass!"

Firelight flickered on the faces of the two men seated in the hall of Tedworth House. There was a pause while the Squire relit his long-stemmed pipe.

"But Squire . . . . ." ventured the other, trying unsuccessfully to keep a straight face.

"And what are you grinning about? Hey?"

"I was thinking. Beg pardon". He stopped again. "I was thinking, that if young Tom Smith lost the action. Who would foot the bill for damages? And legal costs?"

The old Squire died in 1828, we hope in a more forgiving mood. He was regarded as one of the richest commoners in England with an annual income of around a million pounds in modern terms.

The Smiths had lived at Tedworth House since 1650. The first Thomas Smith was a leading international merchant of the City of London and Master of the Skinners Company. Tedworth was a shrewd investment, as money and power were built on woollen cloth, provided by tens of thousands of sheep grazing on Wiltshire Downs. The Napoleonic Wars brought great prosperity to landowners, when England was an island fortress cut off from the continent. But then times changed. Farming became depressed as it tends to do after every war. Also British broadcloth went completely out of fashion.

The Smith family, always resourceful, looked to other ways of making money. Believing in building upon what they already had, they turned to the Llanberis slate quarries inherited from Tom's mother. Slowly, irrevocably, the industrial revolution was raising a head of steam. Factories needed roofs. Slate blocks were called for to make level beds for machines. And thousands of back-to-back houses were built for workers. All these needed Smith's slates.

It became the family rule to spend the summer at Voelas attending to slate business, and the winter at Tedworth. When Tom's father died on 19 May, his son breathed freedom at last!! Freedom to plan and extend his Llanberis empire, together with scope to open up estates in Hampshire.

That autumn, as Tom planned to fashion his country and further the science of foxhunting, frost had touched beech leaves to turn them lemon, pink and copper. Oak leaves felt like paper, and thin sunshine fell on the new Squire's blue coat with brass buttons as he drove to inspect the hundred miles of rides cut, felled, slashed and ripped through the coverts of Faccombe, Doyley Wood, Doles Copse, Harewood Forest and Wherwell. Labourers thankful of the money for bread and beer in hungry years, quarter-sawed oak in sawing-pits with cross-cuts. Andover began to resemble a manufacturing town, or great timber mart, with valuable English oak, ash and chestnut sold by the estate.

The nineteenth century map shows the eastern extent of the hunting country to be much larger than it is today. As well as land surrounding Andover, the boundary marched south-east through Whitchurch to Tidbury Farm, which is near the modern spaghetti-junction of Bullington Cross.

From there it turned westward to follow the little Dever river, with its hatch-holes, water-cress beds and sawmill shallows, until it joins that classic chalk stream the Test. Harewood borders the Test. A river where bright waters harbour the perfect specimen of trout; short and deep, a burnished silver mostly, or yellow-gold with strongly marked spots. Mr. Smith did not like fishing, it was too slow a sport for his fiery temper and restless nature.

If we followed Smith's blue coat worn with buff kerseymere gaiters, he would probably have ridden south, keeping to the west bank of the Test. The shimmering reflection of flat marigold-fields stretching to eternity, were splintered in the mirror water by lines of tall grey poplars. Whether Mr. Smith was moved by the crystal stream we cannot guess. However we know that he had a magnificent eye for fashioning the landscape.

Let us continue the line of his preserves to Mottisfont Abbey, where the

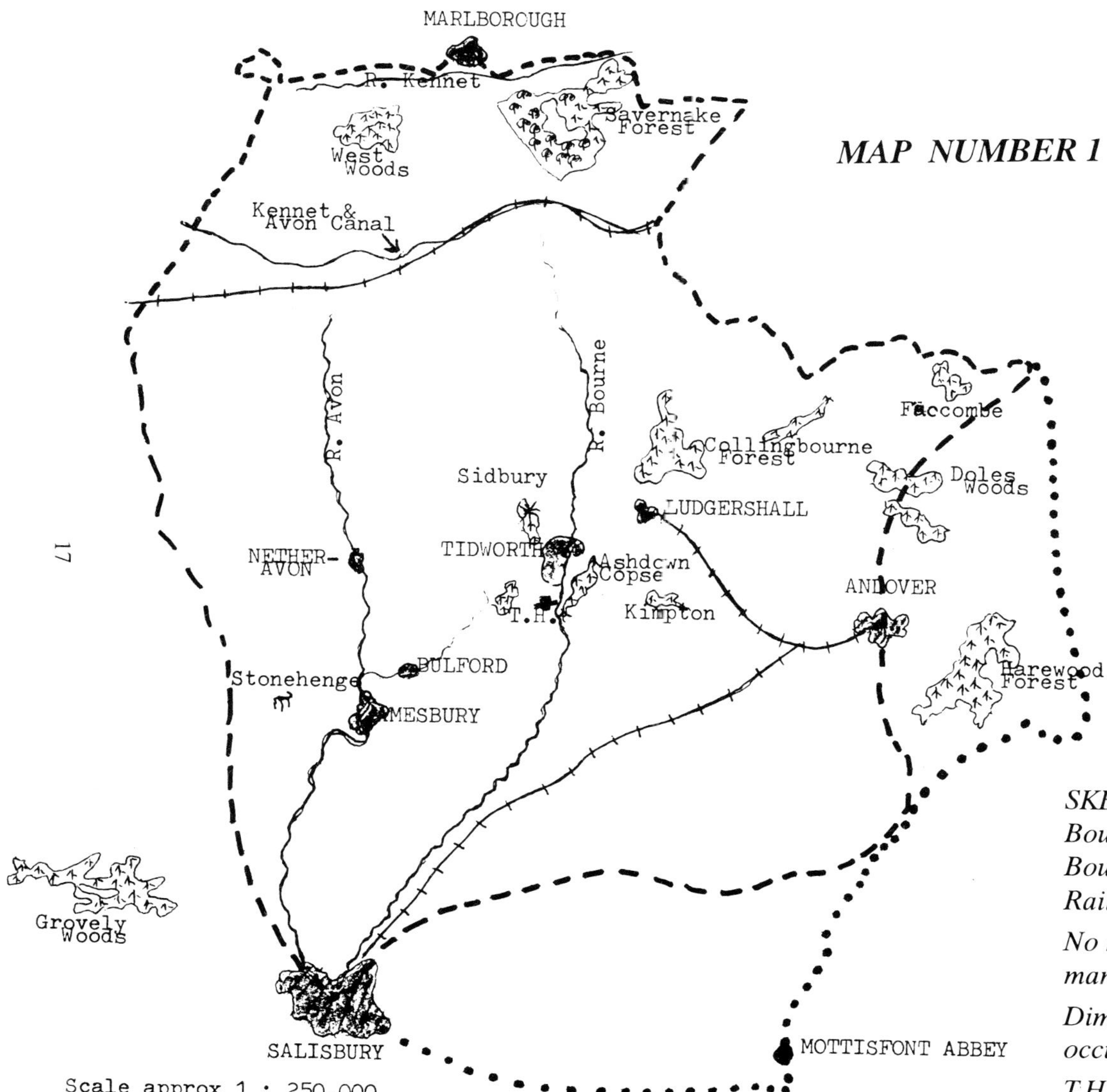

MAP NUMBER 1

SKETCHMAP OF TEDWORTH HUNT COUNTRY

Boundary circa 1828 to 1890 — — — also • • •

Boundary circa 1890 to 1942 — — — only

Railways (some now disused) ┼┼┼┼┼┼┼┼

No roads have been included because routes changed many times during the timescale of the map.

Dimensions of woodland approximate, as changes occurred.

T.H.=Tedworth House.

border with the New Forest Hounds turned abruptly along the line of the Eastleigh and Salisbury Railway shortly to be built. This sweep of country was lent to the Tedworth by the New Forest Hunt, a pack to which Mr. Smith was a constant visitor.[2] His border finally crossed the Bourne river and Salisbury Avon to follow the ancient coachroad which is our virtual boundary today.

Energetic and resourceful, Tom had further plans to rescue the district from lethargic poverty. Like any entrepreneur he wanted a modern house. So he continued to live at Penton for a further two years while he completely rebuilt Tedworth House, the stables and kennels.

Hounds were the first consideration. New kennels were built on the rise within the park, and designed by Tom who drew the plan on a half sheet of paper.* The hound lodging rooms, complete with dished floors, were laid down in compacted clay and chalk. Hounds' sleeping compartments were raised four feet above the ground, and thatched with reed for winter warmth and summer cool. Kennels stood on a small hill, where a delicious greensward sweeps down towards the Bourne river valley. The bronze-blue mass of Ashdown Copse stares across the valley in gloomy contemplation.

To encircle the new kennels a lofty brick wall enclosed a grass paddock for hounds to exercise, or quarrel for supremacy. Hounds are so jealous! And lucky ladies! In the centre of one red wall a pavilion was raised, the only floor from it leading to a shrubbery path from Tedworth House. This meant that visitors had a private grandstand to admire the pack, with no fear of dirty boots, or a paw-marked dress.

Mr. Horlock says that Assheton Smith had a very clever pack mainly of his own breeding. The F.K.S.B. tells us that between 1827-28 he used some of Lord Middleton of Birdsall's sires, many of these hounds being descended from Mr. Corbet's pack who hunted Warwickshire at the end of the eighteenth century.

By 1838 Smith had no fewer than thirty-eight couples by Mr. Horlock's hounds. These were of great size and power, with clean necks and shoulders, good necks and feet, and lengthy frames, many of the dogs standing twenty-six inches in height and the bitches twenty-three to twenty-five. They possessed high courage and spirit, and dashed over stuff which a smaller hound would be obliged to creep through. Being beautiful drawers, the fox must fly, and the thundering crash with which they came down hillsides were quite enough to scare their game away.

The artist who illustrated Eardley-Wilmot's book depicts a romantic Palladian house. Designed in stone,[3] the original entrance on the east side had four columns to support a pediment. The bow-shaped centre-piece on the south was located between two square wings to give the house a rather squat appearance. Solid commercial values of the new middle classes were being reflected in the architecture, as the period started to move from classical Georgian to Victorian years. Essentially the Smiths were astute businessmen. They were solid squires whose fortune was built on expanding trade.

**We do not know for certain the location of these kennels, the kennels in Humber Lane are a later addition.*

There is a second illustration depicting the principal entrance to stables at Tedworth. The working drawing shows Tom's interest, knowledge and attention to detail. Every horse had his own spacious loose-box. And by 1845 we know that fifty horses were in stables, including hunters, carriage-horses and hacks. There were also racehorses and post-horse boxes, all these looked after by an army of grooms, coachmen and boys.

To give us a picture of Tedworth House, let us imagine that it is the first morning in November. Tom and his wife Matilda have recently moved to their new home, and this is the day of the opening meet. Across the park with its carefully ordered groups of ornamental trees, excitement, like fine strings, bonds cloud to trunk writhing down to fallen leaves which toss restlessly in south-west wind. Deer, perhaps a brace of fox, passed by last night and sampled the agitated air with wary interest.

Every lane is crowded with horsemen, dog-carts and carriages all converging for the eleven o'clock meet. Being so far from Bath or London, hunting is a supreme social event, where everyone who thinks they are somebody goes to see, and be seen. The crowd is so vast, there being over four hundred horsemen, together with their wives, families, grooms and coachmen, that Mr. Smith has had two marquees erected in the pleasant, though damp, meadow by the river. One is for farmers, while the other marquee dispenses ale and cheese to servants, estate workers, pedlars, piemen and country girls with ribbon in their hair. Tedworth House and its gardens are reserved for landowners, friends of the family and house guests. It seems probable that the Duke of Wellington himself is a visitor, enjoying a few quiet hours away from the storms and fury of Parliamentary Reform.

A crowd of cutaway red coats with embroidered waistcoats and hunting ties propelled plump ladies between the four Ionic columns which guarded the front door, then on the east side. The women walked slowly into the hall, as corsets were excessive that year to sustain the fashionable shape of short skirts.[4] Shortness of breath, however, was a small price to pay for scalloped crinolines, resembling lampshades, that rose high above ankles clad in striped blue-and-white stockings.

In contrast, a dozen intrepid horsewomen such as Lady Humphrey, or even Lucy Glitters,[5] with weather-beaten eyes below ostrich-plumed hats and wearing velvet hunting-dress, swept past the men into the house. Only women of exceptional stamina and courage, and similar to our international three-day event ladies, could survive the competitive gallops and dare-devil jumps.

The hall was dim. On the Adam-style sidetable six foxes' masks, with ferocious noses, stood in square glass boxes, three a side. They dwarfed the timepiece which said ten o'clock. Knowing Mr. Smith to be a stickler for time, and fearing his violent temper, the impatient crowd pushed into the dining-room, now known as the library.

Candles blazed in candelabra above the long table loaded with trout, salmon and game pies; breasts of pheasant or partridge were decorated with tail feathers. Flushed faces consumed barons of beef, rounds of ham or boar's heads with oranges in their mouths; while spun-sugar delicacies, or ice-cream flavoured with violet seduced the ladies. The noise above great glasses of claret or brandy was deafening. Meantime, somewhere in a draughty passageway the Master was consuming mutton-hash, and planning the day with quiet military precision, before making his entrance.

At precisely eleven o'clock, his hounds greeted Mr. Smith at Tedworth House. Looking at the picture by Fernley which adorned the billiard-room for many years, you can see the impression that Squire made as he rode out to his lawn meet. He rides the extraordinary horse Ayston. Yellow-bay all over, Ayston was pigeon-toed! And this unwarranted thoroughbred had such a bad back that he had to be led to covert. But in a hard run with plenty of deep mud Smith said:

"If I had to ride for my life, I would ride him and no other", so that he refused a thousand guineas for him. He sits in the saddle as though he were part of the horse. And his seat displays vast powers over his frame. He never used a martingale saying:

"My left hand shall be my martingale."

Totally relaxed and standing with a loose rein, the Master is talking to his huntsman and first whipper-in Dick Burton, while favourite hounds Watchman, Commodore, Rifleman and Dimity gaze expectantly into the Master's face. He possessed a fascination over hounds. They would rush towards him, and each morning wait affectionately outside his study window.

The field who were now mounted and breathing breakfast claret, stand respectfully watching England's richest commoner and companion of dukes. The horn blows. And one of the best huntsmen of them all leads to the first draw. He rides past carriages filled with ladies wearing suits in fashionable half-tones or designs blending several colours. Ahead, russet, orange, green and purple leaves fringing new-cut rides through Ashdown, Warren Hill and Kimpton await them. We have no report of the hunt for that day, although several anecdotes tell us about the excellent Ayston.

South Grove Copse lies north of Tidworth, about eight miles distant and near the head of the Bourne river with its numerous tributaries. This dense unyielding covert had been a source of irritation to Tom Smith for several seasons. We must remember that his country was much wetter than it is today, and the modern dry winterbourne river was a network of mud-soaked channels between deep plough. Also that the Enclosure Act of 1835 had not, as yet, affected this part of the West Country, so fields were unfenced and unrestricted for galloping.

The day previous to Tom's determined attack upon South Grove Copse, dozens of men might have been seen trudging around the outskirts with great bundles of furze. Before the Master arrived with forty couple of hounds, black smoke from turf-banked bonfires mingled with a cold steel-grey dawn. Foxes returning from night foraging became anxious. Some broke through the smoke-screen to return to earths, while others raced across the plough towards Grafton Fields.

Meantime the Master shut about twenty couples up in a barn, and for two hours the half pack stirred up those foxes remaining in South Grove Copse. At mid-day Tom launched a second attack, with his fresh twenty couple. Then movement at last! Hounds opened on a dog fox and with joyous music hunted him down the Vale towards Collingbourn* village. The field was off at last. But men soon tired of floundering through mud and pulling horses' tendons. A Mr. Hawkins headed for fresh upland grass of Wexcombe Down, with riders having a steady pull at their horses.

Tom, however, as honest as a schoolboy, kept with his hounds in the impossible mud of the Vale, until his pilot headed towards the higher ground, pointing in the direction of Collingbourn Woods. Presently they came up with the horsemen on the turf, and old Ayston "cut down" every nag amongst them in fair galloping across the Downs, in spite of his exertions in South Grove and Vale mud.

Dick Burton said that the man did not live who could stop Ayston with the Squire on his back, and a fox sinking before his hounds! "Scrutator", alias Mr. Horlock, was less complimentary:

"He was a most fearless, determined performer across country, but I have seen better horsemen, and in my humble opinion he got too many falls. His seat in the saddle was loose, and like that of many enthusiastic huntsmen, who are generally too intent on their hounds to pay much attention to the horse or where he is going. His fearless riding obtained for him the appellation of 'The Hard Gentleman'."

In order to understand the character and achievement of Tom Smith we must follow him to Wales during the summer months, where he managed his 47,000 acre property of Vaenol as an efficient business operation.

The beautiful mansion stood on the sandy shores of Cardigan Bay washed by a silver-grey summer sea. To the south-east high in the sky, the dark overpowering mass of Elidir mountain rises terrace on quarry-blasted terrace two thousand feet above sensational mountain passes. For this is slate country. Grey slate or light blue, dark blue or purple, green and the expensive red slate; all this natural wealth is blasted and dressed, with the slabs manufactured at steam and water-mills. At Tom's father's death many new quarries were opened, until 2400 men and boys were employed processing 1,200,000 tons annually of the best slate to be exported to industrial Britain, Europe and the U.S.A.

Journeying to the mine workings, the view of the black rock (Allt Dû) slate quarries overhanging the upper lake of Llanberis is magnificent. Mount Snowdon rises in the white distance. To the foreground seven terraces, like unconquered ramparts, pile above conical hills of black spoil. The quarries have eaten into the mountain side, while twenty-three miles of tramway harvest slate and slab from the various sites. A bugle sounds in the thin air. The blasting coil, to mine up to 220,000 tons of rock is to be fired. Workmen and boys take shelter, before splinters and huge fragments of mountain are hurled into Llanberis lake below. Today you can visit the Welsh slate museum situated near the lake to commemorate the vast industry powered by men such as Mr. Smith.

To export this wealth the private port of Dinorwic, mid-way between Bangor and Caernarvon, was built on a small scale by Tom's father. His son deepened and enlarged the docks to berth 120 ships against sudden winter storms and the treacherous undercurrents of the Menai Straits.

**The original spelling has been used.*

We can imagine Mr. Smith at Dinorwic standing out to sea aboard one of his five superb yachts. A lonely figure, perhaps he contemplates the design of his first steam yacht, with copper boilers, which was constructed for him at Bristol for £20,000. Or maybe the synopses of his brain spark connections to pattern the design for his prototype yacht with her long hollow water-lines fashioned for speed.

Might his friend the Duke of Wellington stand by his side? They gaze across the grey-green channel towards merchant ships sailing out of Dinorwic, the black mountain increasing the apparent whiteness of languid sailing canvas.

Mr. Smith places the backs of his hands together.

"This," he said, "illustrates hollow water lines. Whereas this . . . ." and he places the palms together, his fingers slightly bent.

"This. Exhibits the normal mode."

His eyes are alight. "Speed. Speed. To transport our ironclad ships faster and more economically to every part of the globe."

The Duke rocks slightly on his heels. Both believe that serious study is the key to rapid advancement.

Ambition? What is ambition? To progress beyond your own limit?

Eardley-Wilmot's book tells us very little about Matilda Smith, except that she had no children, was good to the the needy and had poor health. Tedworth village was managed as efficiently as the business empire. Slates transported south were the obvious material to roof both stone and cob cottages, they also built garden fencing, and hitching posts for horses. The village had four almshouses for the aged and sick maintained by the Smiths, and her husband gave Matilda money to build a school. However, it was not finished until after his death. The school took a hundred children, the girls clad in red cloaks, and was known as "Mrs. Assheton Smith's School".

Every house seems to have had a porch guarded by slates with roses and honeysuckle round the door! It was the romantic garden village! Outside the boundary lived a gamekeeper, his cottage secluded, being approached by narrow paths between minute fields of kale, wheat or turnip, where pheasants and partridge still strut. The cottage was surrounded by a wood. And did his daughter wear a red cloak like Little Red Riding Hood, when she walked to the wood to collect wild berries and pheasant eggs? Eardley-Wilmot only hints that dresses were "not infrequently" given to her by Mr. Smith when a fox was found in the gamekeeper's covert! Or did Mr. Reynard ride a good horse named Fire King.[6] Victorians were experts at insinuating and interpreting fairy tales.

Until now we have concentrated on the district surrounding Penton and Tedworth, but this is only a fraction of the country agreed as Mr. T. A. Smith's. "The Christmas Foxhunter" writing in the *Sporting Magazine* for March 1835 describes a famous run from the osier beds at Amesbury to Salisbury Plain.

The previous year Smith had been in indifferent health, being subject to asthma attacks, although the old 'Hi-Hi' had returned as he rode past the crowds gathered in the parkland of Amesbury Abbey. The meet was at the home of his field Master Sir Edmund Antrobus and was a nine-day wonder.[7]

Completely rebuilt as a grander interpretation of the Duke of Somerset's mansion, six giant Corinthian columns were raised above a porte-cochère

Amesbury Abbey.

on the nine-bay front. Here his hosts awaited him.

Entering through the grand arcade, strange shafts of light filtered from the glass dome surmounting the light-well. The house was even grander than Tedworth. But Smith was a plain man, and he would not have envied his friend's ostentation, especially as the Master was far, far richer. He would have eaten the sumptuous hunt breakfast politely, his thoughts straining towards that first fox, as Antrobus had fine coverts.

Charlie was found amongst the floods and tussocks of the osier beds, a favourite hiding-place, and gave hounds a clipping run. Tom was finding that for the Amesbury type of country a smaller hound was required. The second fox was viewed swimming across the Avon like an otter, and basket-makers straightened their backs from stripping willows, to see the fox breast the opposite riverbank, then shake his brush to the wind, setting his escape towards the dusty uplands.

Meantime horses were forced by the current of the river to retreat to the bridge, surmounted by a Chinese pavilion, half a mile downstream. Two hundred horses would have galloped over the rare and important veranda decorated with chinoiserie trellis, to make wooden posts rattle!

On cold higher ground centuries of charcoal-burning and sheep-rearing have stripped the Plain of trees, leaving chalk-bleached grass to tug against winter wind, which always blows strong and chill. Mr. Smith, riding Golden Pippin, strained wet eyes into the gale to track his pilot forging ahead in the direction of Stonehenge.

You cover the miles when hunting on Salisbury Plain, and it is fast galloping. The thin air makes the psyche see and not see. "Christmas Foxhunter" saw Golden Pippin flag, as he passed the incoherent image of Stonehenge. The trilithons appeared to be writhing as though convulsed by a fit of madness, while coronet stones and corpse stones struggled to pin down a black wraith.

Enticing his horse to go forwards, the large hounds Gay Lass leading

Barmaid and Dairymaid, were showing the way in the direction of Barwick (Berwick St. James). Crossing the ancient coachroad, they were hunting in South and West Wilts country, where courtesy between masters allows you to follow your fox in another's territory. Charles James crossed the Wylye river at Little Wishford and set for Groveley Woods, where women were loading sleighs* with firing on the marshy ground. Taking the trackway up Ebsbury Hill Mr. Smith was alone now, other horses being beat. Hound music echoed from the earthworks right-handed. And the women pressed themselves against their carts as the fox, his brush flagging, hounds and an exhausted Pippin passed by. The pack accounted for their pilot on the Roman road.

"Thank'ee. Thank'ee," said Mr. Smith to the women raising his tall hat. Although his face was pale and drawn.

Quietly hound-jogging home with his breath coming in shallow gasps, the Master met hunt staff and some of the more intrepid field breasting the hill. Stonehenge owned by Sir Edmund Antrobus resembled a battlefield. Sweating horses had either fallen or were burst. A parson suffering from a heavy fall said:

"I wish those confounded Romans had pecked in the ruts before they left this part of the country!"

The decade of the 1830's was troubled by recession. Wages sank to a starvation 12/- (60p) a week. Riots caused 153 men to be sentenced to the gallows from Winchester and Salisbury county courts, with 269 transported for life. In 1833-34 the Tolpuddle martyrs, from a village near Winchester, attempted to form the Friendly Society of Agricultural labourers, and were transported for their insolence.[8]

To crush early seeds of revolt, Mr. Smith became Captain Thomas Assheton Smith by raising his own troop of Yeoman Cavalry. The troop was inspected in Tedworth Park by the Duke of Wellington, with a grand luncheon and fireworks in the evening. Also a picture exists of Captain Smith parading a detachment of beplumed and elegantly caparisoned horsemen in Andover High Street, about 1836. Previous to this, he had lost his Andover seat in Parliament due to his fierce opposition to the Reform Bill although he held his Caernarvon constituency until 1841.

To an autocratic squire who did not like change, let alone reform, these infuriating events probably aggravated the asthma which plagued him all his life.

1842 was a momentous year. By this time Wellington had become enfeebled at an early age, although he still took his daily ride. Visiting Tedworth the faces of the two friends who had experienced so much in common, would have lit up as "The Great Huntsman" George Carter led the Duke of Grafton's hounds on to the lawn. Both he and the famous pack had been bought from the 4th Duke when the country was handed over to Lord Southampton.

With the advent of Carter, Assheton Smith was still to hunt four days a week. But the remaining two were assigned to the new man, with a third pack hunted by him in Wherwell Wood, which was rented from the Vine.

**They were exercising their wood-gathering rights.*

Carter said he had passed enough time in Wherwell to qualify as a parishioner. By 1844 *Baily's Magazine* reported the Duke of Wellington's usual costume as unique:

"A red dresscoat, while trousers made of that horrible invention moleskin, cut short to do duty for breeches, and of course, bagging at the knees, boot-tops brownish and both barely cleaned."

Old age captured Mr. Smith at seventy-eight. Sir Reginald Graham, Bart., in his *Recollections of Foxhunting* speaks of:

". . . . his iron frame was rapidly giving way and the lamp was nearly out."

The old greeting was there, although the old zest for life was gone. And he was forced to hand the horn to George Carter.

The *Salisbury Journal* wrote:

"The Grand Open Day at Tedworth was always signalised by a public breakfast on a grand scale. This sumptuous repast was usually laid out in the dining-room, the splendid gold plate and cups decorating the tables, together with the famed statuette of the Duke of Wellington. These magnificent gatherings were attended by the whole of the neighbouring gentry and yeomanry, and at the last public breakfast in November 1857, when the pack was brought out in front of the house, the worthy squire was surrounded by upwards of six hundred ladies and gentlemen on horseback."

Previous to this in 1845, it was Matilda's health that was giving cause for concern. She was ordered to a warmer South of France climate, and to avoid a painful separation her husband built her a Crystal Palace. This brilliant conservatory saved her life, and was constant source of pleasure for thirteen years.

The scent of orange blossom mingled with lemon and the quiet perfume of carnation. When Matilda entered her conservatory built on the east side of the house, her white hand brushed Italian mimosa, and the yellow sprays collapsed in sympathy. Gaudy bougainvillaea scrambled amongst tree-palms, enjoying the heat from a double row of hot-water pipes. She was able to walk the full hundred yards, ordered by Dr Quinn, before she turned and retraced her steps along the gravel path bordered by thousands of sub-tropical plants. The winter day was dark. But the twinkle of dozens of gas-lamps sparkled through waxy leaves, lit by gas generated at the Gas Cottage near Home Farm.

Seated on a wooden couch supported by cushions, Matilda waited. Shadowy figures distorted by the glass could be seen in an ante-room of the house, glazed on one side and 965[9] feet in length. A chair was brought. Then Buxine, the Squire's favourite mare was led indoors, with the freezing rain beating on a quarter-mile of glass. Slowly he mounted, and at a snail's pace, he rode towards his wife.

Mr. Thomas Assheton Smith died on 9 September 1858 at Vaenol aged 82. His body was brought back to Tedworth and he lies at the Burial Chapel in Church Lane.

Chapter 2

The Marquess, The Parson and Two Huntsmen 1858 - 1878

Tedworth Hunt.

Mr. Smith's will left his entire fortune to Matilda. She returned to Tedworth from Vaenol, although her delicate health forced her to spend the winter with her sisters at Torquay. The mild sea air revived her. But due to the shock of her dominating husband's death, together with a spring chill, she died eight months later on 18 May 1859.[1]

Legend says, that during his Mastership, Mr. Smith accounted for fifteen hundred brace of foxes, although during the last two years of his life he was able to hunt very little, and he kept hounds for his friends' amusement as much as his own. When he died there were ninety couples in kennel, fifty more at walk in Wales and thirty in Wiltshire, besides which he had given twenty couple to the Craven Hunt.[2]

In the November after his death, his wife gave the pack to the county of Hampshire. A committee was formed with the Marquess of Ailesbury as Master and Chairman. George Carter and Jack Fricker were to hunt hounds.[3]

"George," asked one of the field. "Now Squire's dead, how will hounds go on? Without the Squire, I mean?"

Carter sat motionless on his horse, considering. A fine upright fellow.

"Don't see why they shouldn't. Should do very well."

His stern, rather dour expression scarcely altered, as he said,

"If . . . if they've got money enough!"

Then relaxing, his face broke into a warm smile.

"Money. He'd plenty o' that. And he could ride. You see he were a wonderful horseman. But his ways and mine didn't always agree."

Carter made no secret of the fact that he did not regard Assheton Smith as an ubiquitous demi-god!

"You see I liked to find a fox. Have an hour and a half with him. And then kill him, if I could. And somehow or other, I could generally do that. But you understand, Mr. Smith he'd say, "What's the good of caddling about after a fox all day?" And if he hunted one for forty minutes and didn't catch him, he'd try for another. And as soon as he'd tired one horse, he had a fresh one to get on. So it didn't signify."[4]

Eardley Wilmot writing in 1859 tells us:

"There are at present thirty couple of dog hounds in the kennels at Tedworth, and twenty-five-and-a-half couple of bitches. The height of the dogs ranges from twenty-three-and-a-half to twenty-four inch, that of the bitches averages about twenty-two-and-a-half. Mr. Smith found Hampshire needed a smaller hound than Leicestershire."

On December 28 of that year, George Carter being on the sick list, Jack Fricker, the first whipper-in, who had passed his entire life at Tedworth, hunted hounds from Woodbridge.[5] A sporting field, with Sir Edmund Antrobus as field Master, Mr. Studd of Netheravon House, and his wife, an excellent horsewoman, watched Mr. Ferris's withy beds from the bridge over the Avon. As soon as he threw hounds in, Jack announced that pug was at home. Near freezing mist loitered amongst spongy reed, and hounds leapt up as tall as bullrushes which were soaking in iridescent farm-dung water. Patient and persevering, the pack proved honest Jack right when a fine dog fox broke cover towards Woodborough.

Jack, with as many eyes as Argus, watched him pass close by Wilcot. Then turn, to head for the green slime of the Kennet and Avon canal. Boys, throwing stones from the red and blue cabin-roof of a sixty-ton barge, saw the fox slip along above the towpath towards the little bridge of Pewsey wharf. The elder boy allowed his pebble to fall with a desultory 'plop' into the algae-soaked water, crowned with withered sorrel. Pug disdained to tangle his brush with the pea-soup weed, but made for the stone humpback near the loading sheds. Then out of sight below the parapet, the fox crossed the canal to make for Stowell.

The hounds with their short, waxy coats made short work of the marshy ground and hunted him along the high bank bordered with thorn, then tight behind his brush, turned their pilot towards Oare. Such a clatter of horses' hooves there was, as huntsman and hunt staff galloped the bridge. What a pushing and shoving as the big field negotiated the slippery drop-jump by the towpath!

The pace to Draycott Copse was racing. Jack, glad of a few minutes check, viewed his hounds force Charlie out of the leafless cover to Huish, then up the hundred metre high slope towards Coker Wood. In the down-draught of cold December air, the Earthworks crowning the precipice seemed peopled with shades of slave labour who built these enigmatic defences against Saxon invaders, so that Jack's breath quickened with apprehension as spurring his horse on he gained the heights.

Galloping the Earthworks of Huish and Oare hills, frost had tipped thin grass to fine needles, making the chalk cold, hard and heartless. Crossing the Oare-Marlborough road, he reined back, patient and calculating, to contemplate the amphitheatre of tree, grass and rock which surrounds Rainscombe House, two hunted feet below. Hounds descended the escarpment in a white avalanche. Minutes later brown plough separated them into discreet entities, their music magnified in an acoustic basin. The fox paused on yellow-green stubble, in front of a backdrop of elephant-blue tree-belts which blend into the dun-green of Pewsey Down. Gathering his strength, this stout fox raced up the four hundred foot incline of Martinsell Hill, while Jack marked him by galloping Tan Hill Way. Grinning with the satisfaction of a Wiltshireman born and bred, he located his pilot as he negotiated Hill Fort and Pit Trenches.

With superior strength calculated by Mr. Smith to run down any quarry,[6] the hounds hunted well through gorse and coarse grazing of Clench Common towards Savernake (now Park) Farm. At this stage of the hunt, they were entering the country of the twenty-sixth Warden of Savernake Forest..

Sixteen miles of fencing protected red and fallow deer in the Forest, and turnpike roads were gated.[7] At night coaches had to ring a bell for the gatekeeper, at cottages still in existence today on the A4 to Hungerford. But that afternoon hounds and horsemen crossed into Savernake Forest at the three-mile stone from Marlborough towards Andover.

Galloping beside the Column Ride, a deep layer of beech leaves deadened steel horseshoes. Deer had stripped away saplings and low branches, so that rods of winter light emitted a strobe beat to illuminate hounds, now dark, now light, clearly visible through the Park. The pack swerved past a team of Shire horses, pulling a timber carriage which was extracting felled trees. A red squirrel raced up an ash in a rage.

The hunt skirted the pleasure gardens of Tottenham House. George Frederick, the second Marquess of Ailesbury and Chairman of the Tedworth Hunt was unfortunately not in residence to see the brilliant run past his demesne. The handsome Georgian mansion with no Master at home to cheer hounds on, looked with supercilious windows from a series of great reception rooms across grounds where twenty gardeners were barely sufficient to keep winter grass neat and trim.[8] Conservatories, sweet with exotic blossom, which leaned against the orangery, are today cast-iron bones.

The fox, after skirting the walled garden famous for growing fantastic fruits, enveloped for the moment in frost-protecting bundles, broke away towards Timbridge Farm. Bowing to the little Knowle Chapel, the sly one ran the Hungerford road with only low-scenting hounds owning the line. They might have lost him but for a 'Yoi!' from Mr. Sloper. Going to the holloa, hounds and a few intrepid horsemen upended Mr. Sloper's winter wheat, till Charlie was spotted in the turnips. Jack, who could make his hounds draw at any hour of the day with more dash and determination than any professional, nudged the pack to push reynard into the canal. The cold water revived him, and he raced off to Stype Wood, seeking shelter in the courtyard of Standen House.

The huntsman galloping across the meadow heard the cry change. Hounds, knowing they were running a beaten fox spoke a killing pean. Savage. Triumphant. The fox attempted to jump the courtyard wall, but fell back. With mischief and venom in their tongue they accounted for him amongst the bridles, collars and belly bands of the Standen harness room.

During the thirty-two years that Mr. Smith hunted the Tedworth, no subscription of any kind was asked for, landowners being requested only to preserve foxes.[9] William Fawcett in his booklet written for the Hunts Association in 1936 price 1/- (5p) tells us that the Committee of Management was formed during a meeting at the "Star Inn", Andover. The booklet, bound in stiff grey paper, and adorned with the emblem of a scarlet fox is a treasured period piece in the possession of the present Earl and Countess of Cardigan. Advertisements show the "Polly Tea Rooms" in Marlborough as "Open on Sunday from 12.30 p.m.", while the "Haunch of Venison" in Salisbury invites you to lunch and dine.

Committee members were Sir John Pollen, Sir Edmund Antrobus of Amesbury Abbey, the Reverend Henry Fowle of Chute Lodge and Mr. W. Knatchbull, while at a later meeting on 16 November 1860 Admiral Montagu of Stowell and Wilcot was elected, with Mr. J. H. Brewer of Garlogs, near Stockbridge, continuing as Secretary.[10] He had filled that post since time immemorial, and had a very thin wife and a portly daughter. A man of enormous size Brewer was a Master in Chancery and called himself Master Brewer, partly as a lawyer, also perhaps so that people might think he was a Tedworth Master, an honour he coveted! An interfering, pompous fellow he trotted up and down puffing with importance. One day the field lost hounds, in a thick mist on the downs. Then someone saw a large, red object on the distant horizon.

"That's old Brewer. Going over the hill," they said. "Hounds can't be far."

Cheerfully they galloped off. There was Captain Trafford of Stowell, with his cork leg and glass eye. Also little Mrs. Awdry, a tiny lady on a tidy pony. Petite Mrs. Awdry was a witty, accomplished woman, and as they approached the object she had her doubts! Alas, they found no Secretary. Only a large red water-butt![11]

"Well. It's the right shape," she said.

Finance had to be the first consideration with the re-organised Hunt, and a subscription of £1,150 was raised. However, the Marquess of Ailesbury appears to have been the chief financial backer, for the first few years at least.[12]

A valuable Committee Member during the early seven years of his Chairmanship, was the Reverend Henry Fowle. A lifelong friend of Mr. Smith, Eardley-Wilmot tells us that he lived with Tom and Matilda for many years as their greatest friend. People used to have close ties in those days, without the wearisome sexual overtones so adored by modern biographers.

He was never appointed to a parish,[13] inheriting Chute Lodge from his brother William.[14] The estate has several woods and a gorse where foxes are always found. We can picture him dressed in hunting clothes coming down the oval 'flying' staircase below its glass dome. He might have paused to look at portraits of generations of Fowles who lived at the Lodge. Originally the complex at Chute villages were forest settlements hacked out by men with axes beneath the impressive Chute Causeway, a Roman road running from Winchester to Mildenhall.[15]

Henry would have passed through the octagon room with its delicate plasterwork to the library. Opening his letters before the Chute Lodge meet, he might have smiled to hear Mr. Osmond's horse pick its way along the flags at the back of the house. Now Osmond was the butcher from Verham and very fond of hunting. He had a near-blind horse, but he knew the horse and the horse knew him, so they got along somehow. The trouble was that his wife was a very 'tidy' woman, and considered he had better things to do than go fox-hunting, which was why the good man wore his blue smock, and carried a basket of meat for the kitchen.[16] Although a heavy chap he got down from his horse lightly, and Mr. Osmond and meat disappeared to find the cook.

At eleven o'clock George Carter blew to draw the coverts of Longbottom Farm, near Biddesden House, with Osmond, wearing a decent black coat, holding-up on the lane by the two ring coverts south of Chute Lodge! Not so was Parson Gale of Milton, whose coat, cravat and horse resembled Don Quixote's downbeat servant Cevantes.

Today the spire of St. Mary's church appears to rise like an arrow behind the beeches of those elegant rings, set in quiet pasture where sheep graze. The church was built by Thomas Everett Fowle in 1875 in memory of the family. The last heir Michael Randolph Fowle was killed on the Western Front in 1916, aged twenty-one, although his father continued to live at the Lodge for many years and was a long-serving Chairman of the Hunt.[17]

The Chairman after Mr. Smith died was George Fredrick Brudenell-Bruce, second Marquess of Ailesbury 1856-78, and he lived at Tottenham House. His father Charles had rebuilt the mansion, furnishing it with costly Empire furniture from Paris. The house being very much larger, it added to the expense of upkeep and increased the burden on family fortunes.* However Lord Ailesbury lived in princely style as became a Lord Lieutenant of Wiltshire and Knight of the Garter.[18] He gave great entertainments, the Prince and Princess of Wales being among his distinguished guests.

Sadly, only one portrait of him survives. Painted on wood, with a gold tasselled frame, his long, pale face gazes from beneath a Wiltshire Yeomanry shako. Mounted on an impossible stylised bay, because few 'commercial' portrait painters managed to depict true to life horses, his stiff wooden-like leg reminds one of Leech's drawings for Surtees. He commanded the Prince of Wales Own Regiment of Wiltshire Yeomanry Cavalry.[19] And his portrait hangs on the staircase of the present Savernake Lodge.

In 1861 fire destroyed the original Lodge. A very ancient dwelling, from the fourteenth century, it was once a forest ranger's house, probably being a small 'bijou' type residence during Queen Anne's reign. However it was rebuilt about 1780 as a substantial rather rambling demesne, with a large stable block, servant's quarters and coach house.

Early on the Saturday morning of 3 March, a fire started in one of the flues under very suspicious circumstances. The *Marlborough Times* said on 16 March 1861:

"We are sorry to announce the entire destruction of Savernake House,** one of the seats of the Marquess of Ailesbury. The fire was discovered about 5 a.m. by the gardener, who was sleeping in the house. The noble marquess and marchioness were at the time with a select circle of friends staying at Tottenham-park.*** The progress of the flames was so rapid that nothing but a portion of the furniture could be saved, the entire mansion being completely burnt down by 10 o'clock, only five hours from the first discovery of the fire."

**Hawtrey's School until 1994*

***renamed Savernake Lodge.*

****renamed Tottenham House.*

The "Sun Insurance Office" paid out the sum of £3000 in compensation.

Today only a black and white stable block surmounted by a clock-tower remains, together with a curious pavilion-like structure built at right-angles to it. This is the modern Savernake Lodge. You pass under an archway and broken hands of the double-sided clock no longer tell you the time. A geometric herb-garden, set in gravel, scents the dining room windows, where a trio of Brudenell-Bruce daughters wearing crinolines, pearls and silk grace a wall converted from eighteenth-century loose-boxes. Past the drawing-room a strange long passage links house to pavilion. Here water falls softly into a stone basin and plants nestling in gravel shed a luminous green light.

Further rooms have curious tracery windows. Was the last one a servant's hall for the burnt mansion? Or a counting-house? This final hall now a billiards room, with its vaulted ceiling, gazes out on to a damp lawn, thick with moss. Garden steps lead nowhere. Dark trees mark out the square of "The Ruins".

Legend has it that on the morning of the fire a servant passing the house heard a tremendous crash. He saw flames, but did not raise the alarm. They say that the present Lodge remembers the blaze. About the third of March, there is a high wind with a phantom creaking and crashing. And like a Chinese mystery, roof timbers give such a squeaking and groaning in unison with the tempest-image.

Later hunt cards printed "The Ruins" for the venue of a meet in Savernake Forest.

In 1865 Lord Ailesbury took a more active part in the management of the Hunt and followed Sir Edmund Antrobus as field Master.[20] One wonders if the field were commanded with military precision, together with the pride and efficiency of a regimental manoeuvre. Because like his uncle the Earl of Cardigan of Crimean War fame, Ailesbury was no mere figurehead. However, due to a violent disagreement with the War Office, he resigned as Colonel of the Wiltshire Yeomanry Cavalry in 1876, to die, very generally respected a couple of years later.[21]

1865 was an eventful year as it was agreed that the loaned New Forest country from Speary Well to Clarendon be given up. Also the Reverend Henry Fowle died and George Carter, who had hunted hounds since 1842 retired, handing the horn to his first whipper-in Jack Fricker. Unsurpassed as a huntsman, he settled at Milton Lilbourne, and had a very comfortable house with stabling, yards and about six acres of good pasture. He also had a nice easy Galloway kind of horse, sent to him by his son Andrew[22]

Although highly thought of when hunting hounds, Carter was not without faults! Imperious at home, he was subject to occasional outbreaks of temper. His children, as well as the woman who called him husband had a lively time of it, if they did not turn to the old huntsman's 'holloa' as quick as they might have done! On the hunting field George always appeared in a black frock coat, properly cut and a high hat. He only wore his red coat on his birthday.

One wonders if he were out on 6 February 1871 when "Nascitur Nonfit" in *The Field* described a brilliant run after a long hard frost. Mrs. Josceline the 'graceful Amazon' was in fine form, with formidable women such as Lady Humphrey of Penton riding her favourite King of Trumps, together with other ladies from the adjacent Beaufort Hunt. Nor were men such as Messrs. Raikes, Marsh and Captain Tyson slacking. A fox was disturbed in Everleigh Ashes, and the field raced over springy turf, until once past Easton Wood you enter the Vale.

Very different work now. The pace slows a bit as the fences are big, and clay-mud heavy. Hounds gallop straight. However a few of the men and some of the ladies go scrupulously straight rather than ride the road. After a check at Durley, the pace is racing again to Savernake Forest, where the carpet of dead leaves is treacherous with people singing out "'Ware bog!"

Our own horses are schooled to bend serpentlike through Savernake trees. But the forest echoes and resonates with screams from Beaufort ladies, their veils snagged on whipping branches, skirts speared by saplings. The shrieks from the screaming ladies are perhaps in titillation, excitement surpassing terror. The hounds are off again for a complete run of fifteen miles running over a course of twenty-five, in two hours and thirty minutes. Or so they say, before accounting for their fox!

About 1878 Carter's sight began to fail, so he gave up hunting because he was afraid to go where he could not see well. He was devastated. But his sadness softened his temper, as though bowing to the inevitable and he died in his ninety-second year.

Thus by 1879 the Marquess and the Huntsman pass into history.

Chapter 3

Jack's Three Masters and the Rector of Mildenhall 1879 – 1899

Tedworth House 1880.

It must have been a Wednesday or Friday because the new Master, Sir Reginald Graham (1879-82), of Netheravon House, was hunting hounds from a meet at Collingbourne Shears. Jack Fricker hunted the pack on Tuesdays, Thursdays and Saturdays, and did not normally come out on a bye-day[1]

Hounds had been hunting a great circle around Ragged Appleshaw all the morning, then on to Chute Causeway as far as Scot's Poor. Back again they came, hunting the same fox by way of Chantry to Collingbourne Wood, forcing him out by Crawlboy's Farm. Their pilot led them across Ludgershall Common, through Mr. Young's Plantation to the top of Tedworth Hill, where there were two lines and he beat them.

Sir Reginald felt that this was not good fox-hunting country, or indeed good scenting country. And the endless flints cut hounds' feet, causing a deal of trouble in kennel. But it was one of the best for foxes he had ever known. He could find them everywhere.

Although not out with hounds, Fricker might have been on exercise that day, and we can picture him standing on the five hundred-foot high main ride which bisects Ashdown Copse. His quick ear would have heard the cry, and told him hounds were coming that way. From his vantage position, he guessed they had found again on Sidbury Hill. The music dispersed as they negotiated the Earthworks, then sounded joyous and clear from Dunch. Hunting on unseen for ten minutes, Jack might have picked them up again as they worked their way across the snow-scattered Tedworth House parkland, which lay on the far side of an icy stream and some hundred and fifty feet below him.

Although there was a bond of mutual respect between Master and huntsman, Jack was a worried man. Sir Reginald was an excellent sportsman, having been Master of the Cotswold between 1871-3 and the New Forest from 1874-8[2] Unfortunately Jack knew Sir Reginald thought he might have been an even better huntsman had he gained experience in other countries, rather than serving at Tedworth all his life.[3] So who was to hunt the beloved pack in future? Would he be superannuated?

A momentary ray of February sunlight hit the newborn Kelk coat-of-arms on the central pediment of the re-modelled House. Sir John Kelk buying Tedworth in 1876 had brought in an army of workmen to erect Portland stone columns and slabs of sculptured masonry, so that by 1878 Assheton Smith's mansion had been almost totally replaced,[4] although hounds were still lodged at Mr. Smith's model kennels,[5] where Jack lived. Sir John was a good friend to the Hunt. The sun moved upward past the original front door, now the ballroom reaching to a giant 'K' below the palatial clock-tower[6] Meantime Jack, who could distinguish most of the hounds by tongue,[7] heard the pack gain the demi-mount above the wall of trees behind the House. Here pastry-like snow gave up the fox from the turnips, and hounds raced for the gentle escarpment of Dunch Hill.

Jack picked his way down the steep track towards the river. In a warm bowl of the Copse sheltered by thirty-foot laurels, pussy-willows inspected melting snow to see if early violets were breaking through. He might have grimaced on hearing an explosion of branches and twigs as Sir Claude de Crespigny, a horseman of iron nerve, plunged headlong down the ravine to breast ice-floaters in the water.

"There goes Sir Claude again! Never did know if a gate be open or shut!"[8]

Listening intently, Jack could have heard the cry rise a pitch as hounds U-turned to hunt the black beechwoods of Clarendon Hill. The passionate cry made him gallop along the gravel road past St. Mary's church, completed that year in rock-faced brown stone. Only a civil engineer such as Kelk could have designed a cylindrical tower and spire to look like a valve on a steam-engine.[9] But Jack was not a chap to notice such niceties!

A party of horsemen had caught up, and he led them through the small village, passing Mrs. Assheton Smith's school at Hampshire Cross. Turning left-handed, they passed front gardens where they saw caps tugged at, and sacking aprons bobbed, because people were deferential. Men were sometimes surly and often afraid. Besides, all riders look alike in high hats, thus nobody knew if the noble Duke of Somerset were passing or even Squire Hicks-Beech. And dismissal could be immediate and absolute.

They cantered the greasy chalk track up Clarendon Hill. Black ice plastered the five hundred-foot summit. Looking west towards Netheravon where Sir Reginald had his house, Jack felt the silence of the Downs. Under a liquid metal sky half snow, half melt, the sweeping rise and fall of the land resembled the waves of an ocean. There was mile upon mile of swelling surface, with nothing to break the scene or hide the view. In the near foreground the field was galloping the mud and cattle of Zouche Farm. Then through the Pennings to the earths of Sidbury Hill.

If, as they say, clay like a magnetic disc is stamped with the talk of men, so prehistoric Sidbury Hill camp must have recorded Tom Smith's voice as he hunted his rabbit-beagles as a boy. Now hares are a pest to any huntsman. And in the banks of the camp, Jack had seen an hundred hares leaping thorn and scrub. He was confident his hounds would never look at a hare while puzzling a line. But he must have been concerned that his new Master might hunt hounds himself. And deprive Jack of his authority.

Knowing there was always a long wait at Sidbury, he rested in the saddle. The sun was low in a mauve sky. Suddenly knives of mist hard and sharp began to form in the hollows. As he watched, they drove across the downland with insistent speed, threatening a foggy afternoon.[10]

"And I reckon that's that for today! If he's wise," said Jack to himself, "Master'll need that compass of his, if he's to sleep in his own bed."

Jack was probably right. There were no roads from Sidbury to Netheravon, only a confusing network of tracks past cottage wells and Figheldean Fields. Carriage wheels were impossible and horses the only transport.[11]

Damp clings to the thin clay cap covering the chalk. Gorse, sheep and rabbits inhabit the Downs. But Netheravon valley in summer is green, pastoral and sweet. Downs give way to pasture along the sides of the wide Avon river which serves a string of villages from Upavon to Salisbury. Here fruit grows and vegetables flourish.

Sir Reginald Henry Graham, eighth baronet of Norton Conyers, had rented Netheravon House from Sir Michael Hicks-Beech for three years.[12] The handsome Georgian mansion is perched on a knoll above the village, which stands on a loop of the Avon. The river divides into small streams. And tiny tributaries, some natural, some made-made, join and rejoin in flowery water-meadows fringed with pollard willow.

Sir Reginald was a keen fisherman and rented the fishing rights.[13] Not a true chalk stream like the Test, it is a late river. Avon fish are seldom in condition until the end of May. From June to September he was seen wading shallows between bog-green pastures. Tranquil cows ate in a vista of wide fields. Even in summer cold downwinds from Salisbury Plain which rises high above the Avon can be treacherous to a man's health.

On Monday 15 November 1880 hounds met at Netheravon House and a large field turned up, amongst them were Lord Algernon St. Maur, Lord Lawrence, Lord Wiltshire, Sir William Humphrey, Sir Edmund Antrobus and Hon. Percy Wyndham (the next Master) with Mrs. and Miss Wyndham.[14]

Refreshments were served on the terrace where beech and elm had been stripped of leaf by wind from the Plain, but cypresses, still growing today, decorate the neo-classical front of the house, with its white portico. At the rear stands an extensive stable block. The house is now an officers' mess of the Support Weapons Wing.

Ladies' fashion. That sensitive comment on social aspirations was on a cusp, and hardly knew where to look for inspiration! The immense prosperity of the 1850's age of extraordinary wealth and brilliant luxury, welled up during the 1870's. Benjamin Disraeli, the Jew who rose to be Prime Minister, popularised the Imperial ideal in England, and never had any age been so good! On Netheravon lawn in 1880, riding habits had long tails with vents in the basques of the jacket. But even Sir Reginald with his slightly balding forehead and wide-set eyes might have had difficulty in keeping a straight face!

His photograph shows he had a pleasant smile.[15] Walking between ladies with their enormous bustles, on which you might balance a dinner-plate, his soft brown eyes must have noted a feminine passion for dead animals, real or imitation. A widowed Queen dressed in hideous black, and an ominous military defeat to come at Majuba Hill did nothing to deter fine ladies wearing a whole aviary of birds, complete with eggs, in their hats. Dresses were decorated with beetles, cockchafers, centipedes, lizards and scorpions. Also rats, mice, snakes, spiders and flies. And what could the Master say to a dress trimmed with cats' heads? Or one with imitation mice from bosom to hem?[16] Lord Algernon St. Maur with his thin shoulders, spindly legs in creased breeches, and high hat above a pale, bald, aristocratic face, must have said:

"Stuff and nonsense!"

Hounds moved off at half-past eleven with Fricker, John Bevan and Jack Thatcher whipping-in. They drew one of the coverts above the Avon rented by the Master, and instantly a brace of foxes was on foot. One raced over the water-meadows up to Fittleton village, with hounds very handy to him, then he set his head straight for the Downs until he was turned by a team of horses and caught in the open near Upavon. The pace was pretty good, five miles in thirty-five minutes.

They found another fox in a turnip field, and gave him a good dusting for twenty-five minutes until he was lost in a storm near Wilsford. Meantime the Master was not a happy man. In Chirton Gorse, a capital covert on the steep side of Salisbury Plain, a deluge of rain ended the day.

For Sir Reginald soaking clothes brought on a severe attack of sciatica, the result of wading for trout during the autumn! And he missed many hunting days.[17]

So perhaps Jack need not have worried after all!

The Master was a great hound man. Since Mr. Smith's day when his enormous hounds could rest their muzzles on the breakfast table licking their chops at his mutton hash, the pack was being bred smaller and lighter. Fashions in hound breeding had revolutionised.

We know that Sir Reginald had foxhunting bred in him, and was a friend and pupil of Lord Henry Bentinck, who hunted the Blankney country, and would have no "soft" blood in his kennel. Lord Henry favoured light, racy hounds for stamina, and those who kept their speed until late in life. He spoke of bone as that "useless appendage", any excess tending to slow up a hound and fatigue him.

While Master of the New Forest we know Sir Reginald bought seventy couple of Craven hounds. Also Mr. Chaplin, who succeeded Lord Henry, gave him eighteen couple from the Blankney. Therefore it seems logical to presume that Sir Reginald would have favoured this type of light, fast hound for the Tedworth.

Returning to the northern part of our country, the railway from Hungerford through Savernake to Devizes was opened to public traffic on 11 November 1862. The *Marlborough Times* describes it as a "compact little station containing first and second class waiting, retiring rooms all neatly fitted up and complete in every respect. Except for one thing! No refreshment room!"[18]

This omission would have scarcely concerned the noble Duke of Beaufort as he stepped from the train at Pewsey station in the spring of 1882. Doubtless an epicure collation awaited his Grace after hunting as he and his companions the Marquess of Waterford and Lord Arthur Somerset rode to meet the Duke's hounds at Clench Common.

That morning food and Mr. Burton's excellent ales were very much on the minds of lesser mortals for the meet at the Brewery, East Kennet. The waiting crowd jostled for free beer, and to eye the brilliant blue and buff cutaways, mingling with red coats of the Tedworth. The Marquess of Worcester, who became ninth Duke and Master in 1899, was hunting hounds by invitation of Sir Reginald, who was to retire that season.

The Marquess did not wait long at the Brewery, but led hounds to meet the Duke's party five miles away. It was said that the field grew like a snowball. Horsemen and carriages, both fashionable and yeomen, waited at every corner. Sadly, hunting did not live up to expectations. Charlie was not at home on Clench Common, and a friendly earth ended a short hunt to Wick.

Then they tried Wernham Gorse, where a fox jumped up in the middle of the pack, raced through Brick-kiln Coppice, and down the vale in the direction of Wootton Rivers. He turned right towards Broomsgrove, and again mounted Martinsell Hill into Clench, where he was lost.[19]

After that the Tedworth was without a Master until the Hon. Percy Scawen Wyndham, third son of the first Baron Leconfield, of Clouds, East Knoyle, Wiltshire, took the horn, 1882-1885. Percy Wyndham was M.P. for West Cumberland between 1860-85.[20] Hunting in Wiltshire, he lived at Wilbury, near Fosbury, which is on the north border of our country, being south-east of Savernake Forest.

He has left us no written notes, although Sir Reginald tells us that in the Wilbury district Lady Charles Wellesley lived at Conholt Park. She was an excellent preserver of foxes, and her two sons, Henry and Arthur, were keen on the chase. Later they both became Dukes of Wellington, while Sir Richard Sutton and his son Ted, of Benham Park, were occasional visitors from the Craven.

At Wilcot Manor, south-west of Savernake, lived Lord Algernon St. Maur, afterwards the fourteenth Duke of Somerset. This area, bordered by the Roman road of Chute Causeway to the south, the upper reaches of the Avon river to the west and the lovely hills of Oare and Huish leading to Savernake, is the most beautiful part of the county. At a meet at Oare, the first fox after a great run sought refuge in Marlborough College. Entering by the Master's garden, Charlie bolted through a passage into the quadrangle and took shelter in the racquets' court!* Here two young gentlemen were at play. The fox crossed court! While hounds, red coats, black coats, high hats and ladies in long tails, hardly observing such euphorisms scattered balls, racquets and boys till the fox was despatched, and the mask presented to a master, Mr. C. M. Bull. He was delighted, and

**Was this the small court used before the racquets court was built?*

had the mask mounted for the College museum.[21]

Wyndham resigned the Mastership in 1885 as other duties proved too onerous for him to continue. He became High Sheriff of Wiltshire in 1896, besides being a J.P. and D.L. for the county.

His photograph shows a bullet-headed man with a high forehead. Seated in his library on a substantial chair, one hand is looped over the carved mahogany arm. The fingers of the other are extended in contemplation of weighty matters.[22]

Records say little about Mr. F. Vaughan Williams, Master 1885-88, except that hunting was reduced to three days a week. Foxes became difficult to find, as shooting was inevitable. No hunting! No preservation! Therefore no foxes!

Fortunately we can learn about our country thanks to the scores of letters preserved by Alfred Soames, third son of Reverend Charles Soames, of Mildenhall. The letters were written by the family while he farmed in South Africa.*

Reverend Charles Soames does not seem impressed with Vaughan Williams. He observed on 29 December '85:

"The Master not out today. Rather a poor creature I'm afraid."

Although brother Charles, his son, writes on 9 February '86:

"Vaughan Williams a nice chap. Pretty little wife. Quite a girl!"

While a month later George tells his brother:

"The Tedworth met at Collingbourne for Southgrove to finish the season. Vaughan Williams does not know his way about the country a little bit. He generally comes by train as he does not like long rides or long days."

The last excerpt is a wonderful comment on the way the country was being opened up by railways.

Mildenhall House stands by the main road on a small hill above the village. Originally the incumbent had one hundred and fifty acres of glebe land, with four sheep, two cows, bullocks, a small dairy and three horses. But Mrs. Soames did not like the rectory. The bishop agreed to their building another home provided:

"It was a good house. Built on good land!"

Luckily he does not seem to have been an anti-hunting bishop!

An elegant house, it is built of red brick incorporating imaginative glazed Dutch brick, which gives it a rich shine in the sun. Cast-iron pillars support a white verandah, where the family sat at tea to overlook the Kennet river meandering a quiet way in the shallow valley between willow trees. The family grew and grew. Very soon the parson had to raise the roof to build on another storey. Census records show six sons and six daughters, together with nannies, a governess, cook, housemaids, 'tweenies, all living together under the raised slate roof. You can still see the Portland stone line supporting the original rafters. The geometric garden of interlocking triangles, designed by the rector's wife, is filled with tulips and forget-me-nots. A royal red deer guards the front door beneath a pillared stone arras. Captain Stanning, R.N. (retired), former bursar at Marlborough College,

These letters were deciphered, typed and collated with infinite patience by Mrs. Lucy Judd, grand-daughter of Reverend C. Soames.

and his charming wife welcomed us to tea and history.

Rectory ladies wore tailor-mades and sewed good works in the drawing-room near the winter fire, surrounded by blue and white Delft tiles. By 1886 lounge suits had arrived for men. George sitting in the large bay window with shutters writes:

"I had seven days' hunting. But only one good day. Otherwise either mangy foxes or bad scent.

All the other days I had with Lord Savernake's yellow coats, and turned a stag out on Shalbourne Hill."

George Frederick, second Marquess of Ailesbury, was succeeded by his brother Ernest. By 1878 there was a great dearth of cash in the family coffers, the country moreover was suffering an agricultural depression, so the new Marquess had to go very carefully indeed.[23]

Even at Mildenhall we learn:

"Wheat makes 14/- (70p) a quarter. Lambs 15/- (75p) each. Farms were let at very low rents. Mrs. Tucker's by the "Shepherd's Rest Inn" used to make £600. Now let at £100."

Ernest was succeeded by *"The Black Sheep"*, William Brudenell-Bruce, fourth Marquess of Ailesbury, 1886-94. However, at the time of Gordon's letter on 28 January he was still Lord Savernake.

"The staghounds are very little bigger than beagles. The babbling brutes go towling about giving tongue on every possible opportunity. They run everything they come across. However, Lord S. likes the amusement, and he attires himself in a smart coat, canary coloured, swears at the field, and does an immense amount of drinking. He goes to the "Public" and treats the farmers to champagne.

"Being a heavyweight he is not active enough to vault from horse to horse. To enable him to mount more easily the horse is instructed to stretch itself out as though to stale. Rather absurd for a man of two and twenty."

On 15 September another brother, Ward, writes:

"Lord Savernake and three of his friends were caught by the exciseman without game licences."

From 1888-98 the Mastership of the Tedworth was taken by Mr. Charles Peyto Shrubb, of Merrist Wood, near Guildford. The *County Gentleman* of 1884 describes Shrubb, as a young lad, as paying:

"More attention to the Goddess Diana than was good for the acquirement of the classics!"

Before coming to us, he had previously hunted the Burton, as well as the Ripley and Knaphill Harriers.[24] It is interesting that he followed both Sir Richard Sutton and his great friend Mr. Assheton Smith at the Burton, although his Mastership was after the division into Burton (North) and Blankney.

In 1877 Shrubb built a richly timbered house of neo-Elizabethan design and generous proportions by the architect Norman Shaw. The house was at Merrist Wood, owned by the family since 1770, and is now an agricultural college.[25] During the hunting season Mr. Shrubb lived at the Oaks, near Andover.

On 28 August Jack Fricker died. They say he had a sad end. From the

Merrist Wood Hall, the home of Mr. C. P. Shrubb, M.F.H. 1888-98

thin lad riding a carthorse bareback, he rose to become one of the finest huntsmen. After his death a testimonial was collected, which was invested in London and South Western Debenture Stock. The interest was paid to his wife during her lifetime, and afterwards to his daughter.[26]

Mr. Shrubb was a very good and popular Master and did everything well, bearing most of the expense personally. With Fricker dead, he hunted hounds himself. To begin with Bevan was first whipper-in with J. Goater as second, but 1891 saw Fred Perrin the kennelhuntsman, whom he brought with him, turning hounds to Mr. Shrubb after Bevan's departure. The Master was a great houndsman, and they hunted four times a week.[27] Unlike Vaughan Williams, he rode everywhere! Even when trains were available he did not use them.

Once again he took over the New Forest country formerly loaned but given up in 1865, and also Wherwell Wood. Wherwell was a home of foxes! And not hunted since Mr. Smith's time. Shrubb knew that if hunted persistently foxes would lie out of covert and give good hunts.

A charming photograph of a lawn meet is still in existence.[28] It is late autumn, and the elegant house may be the Oaks, Andover. Well-bred hunters are posed in a semi-circle, with Master and excellently controlled hounds standing centre. Two fashion-plate ladies each riding side-saddle, their heads slightly forward to exemplify composed beauty, are arranged each side of Mr. Shrubb. Only five other men are mounted, perhaps staff who may comprise Charles Shrubb, Fred Perrin and J. Goater, together with two other friends. The ensemble suggests this is an exclusive morning meet, and posed picture.

The hounds are very interesting. Supported by the *Foxhound Kennel Studbook records,* we think they are Belvoir-type. Major Jonathan Seed, M.F.H., R.A., believes this is borne out by their being 'square' hounds, and that they are a little 'fine with short heads'.

Hounds were Shrubb's great love. As Master for a continuous period of ten years, he was able to breed from favourite hounds and keep to his own line, rarely seeking blood from other packs. The F.K.S.B. for 1896 says that Mr. Shrubb used the famous Brocklesby Acrobat '90, by Belvoir Grappler

'85, on his Gravity '91. However, the sole progeny Gamesome does not appear to have been bred from. Litters from two sires of Lord Radnor's pack were also used, but neither contributed puppies to the kennel.

His son, Mr. Charles Shrubb, practically fulfilled the duties of whip in the field. In the latter end of 1899, the Master's health began to fail and he died the following year. Charles acted as Master until the end of the season. Mr. Shrubb was exceedingly popular, and as a mark of esteem in which he was held, the members of the Hunt presented him with a silver model of his favourite horse, Insurance, the winner of several great races.[29]

Chapter 4

Mr. Yorke Scarlett and The Royal Regiment 1899 - 1906

Small seeds may presage distant repercussions! That year 1898 saw two unrelated events, firstly the acquisition by the War Office of forty-five thousand acres of Salisbury Plain area,[1] and secondly the advent of Mr. Hussey's Netheravon Harehounds. Of passing mention in themselves, maybe it was fortunate that Mr. Shrubb during his last months of life was unable to visualise future consequences.

Whether he actually attended the mass manoeuvres from 1-8 September 1898 at Boscombe Down is not known, although he must have read excited newspaper accounts of the march past by fifty thousand troops.[2] Also the description written in verse and entitled *"Mrs. Brown at the Review"* published and sold for one penny:

"We've bin up top o' Boscombe Down.
About three mile fro' Amesbury town,
An' there we seed a splendid sight,
A hundred thousand soldiers quite
A-marching by so gallantly."

Apparently free beer had brought on double vision when counting numbers.

The blunders of the Crimean War alarmed everyone. While the Franco-Prussian War of 1870 created further apprehension, so the cry throughout the army was:

"Give us the men, and *an area to train them on.*"

After the passing of the Military Lands Act in 1892, the Government was given powers of compulsory purchase on land required for training purposes. A pressing need was for an extensive tract of empty land to carry out army manoeuvres, and Salisbury Plain was considered suitable because it is about a hundred thousand acres of poor downland rising to seven hundred feet. Roughly circular, the area occupies the heart of Wiltshire with direct road and rail access to London. It is divided north to south by the river Avon, its dry, well-drained soil is suitable for cavalry and horse-transport. Furthermore its poor quality grassland supported thousands of hurdled sheep confined to sheepwalks. The sparse population lived in small villages grouped in the fertile valley of the Avon, or by the tiny winterbourne river Till. Land to the east of the Avon towards Tidworth was smiling, pleasant plough and woodland.

Between 1897 and 1899, forty-five thousand acres were bought by the Secretary of State as a permanent training ground for calvalry, infantry and gunners (later this acreage was doubled).[3] Tedworth hunting country extends as far as the medieval coachroad linking Salisbury with Foxley Corner. Here it abuts the South and West Wilts domain.[4] Thus a goodly portion of traditional hunting area was now owned by the military, but with as yet little clash of interest. It was not until fifty years later that occupation of Salisbury Plain Training Area land was to become a source of sad conflict.

Meets on the cold, high chalklands where winds blow keen and cold, and flocks of Wiltshire Horned sheep grazed under curlew skies, were few, because there was a great deal of soft pastoral country to enjoy. This in spite of Bulford, Haxton and Figheldean Fields together with Tidworth village falling into the hands of the War Office. A greater worry was that although roads had little traffic, railways criss-crossed England like an untidy spider's web,[5] and soldiers mean rail transport. Barbed-wire was also becoming a hazard, being cheaper for depressed farmers to erect than well-laid hedges and jumpable ditches.

The second incident mentioned was the advent of Mr. Hussey's Netheravon pack of harehounds, kennelled at his home the Old Brewery, and exercising above the water-meadows of Netheravon House, compulsorily bought by the War Office to the immense chagrin of Sir Michael Hicks-Beech. Since the hare is hunted by courtesy of master of foxhounds, the new pack founded in 1899[6] was a welcome addition to the sporting fraternity. Brigadier-General Hope cites fifty-eight harrier packs working in Hampshire during the eighteenth and nineteenth centuries, with a further three using beagles[7]. Strangely there were few harriers in Wiltshire, so cheerful Arthur Hussey and his hounds were eagerly accepted.

While gunners fired rounds propelled by cordite from Bustard towards Redhorn Hill or Casterley Camp, fate said that the new young Tedworth Master should be the son of Lieutenant Colonel W. J. Scarlett, Scottish Division Garrison Artillery. Further, that no fewer than five of his cousins, including a brace of Major Generals, would serve as Royal Regiment officers. All gunners together![8]

They made a happy pair, the energetic Laird of Gigha, William James Yorke Scarlett and generous Arthur Edward Hussey. As Yorke Scarlett was to be associated with us for the next half-century, let us look at his family and history in some detail.

Sugar plantations in Jamaica were the basis of the Scarlett fortune, when Robert of Duckett's Spring, aptly named, married the daughter of Philip Angling of Paradise. This estate was unlikely to have been heavenly bliss for African slaves, but excellent for cane sugar profits. Their fourth son was Chief Justice of the island, and he increased the family income by marrying a Welsh heiress to a sweet West Indian fortune[9]

By 1838 sales of cane sugar had collapsed when well-crystallized beet-sugar was produced at Northampton, Massachusetts, U.S.A. The next generation, James William, returned home to practise as barrister-at-law in Sussex and county Argyll.[10]

But the call of the Gulf Stream, curling around Jamaica and the Mull of Kintyre alike, lured Yorke Scarlett's father to retire from the army and buy Gigha in 1865, a strange exotic island floating off-shore from gentle Kintyre towards Islay and Jura, where winter is not severe and spring comes quickly.[11] Succeeding as Laird at sixteen, Yorke Scarlett acquired a pack of harriers which he hunted for his own unshared amusement from the azalea gardens of Achamore House and alongside the white sandy shores of Gigha Sound's turquoise sea. Today you can walk on paths and trails all over the island using gates specially constructed so that the first rider could flick off the latch with his whip.[12]

But he grew tired of solitude, and pined for greater things. For two seasons he became Master of the Craven hounds, and when Mr. Shrubb died took over our hounds, hunting four days a week from his first home at Etwell House, and afterwards from Fyfield, near Andover.[13]

Meantime, Arthur Hussey's family stayed at home. They were brewers of Netheravon, although Hussey's brewery ceased about 1890. The house stands by a narrow lane off High Street, and leads to empty desolate kennels. Stables stand behind the house on the opposite side of the lane, and were originally built for drayhorses which pulled the great flat waggons, equipped with iron-shod wheels, and loaded with beer barrels. The date 1899 inscribed above the barred windows of the stables, most likely records the year the brewery was sold. Small blue tiles, used to pave the yard, may still be seen behind the carpenter's shop, where years ago a doctor had his surgery.[14]

Although the War Office had purchased Sir John Kelk's 6,618 acre property including thirteen farms, eight farmhouses, a hundred and seven cottages and the Ram Hotel in North Tidworth for £95,000, hounds were still kennelled at Tedworth House.[15] The downs were still downs, and as yet, not churned into a mud morass by army vehicles, nor tangled into birdcages of wire. When Yorke Scarlett lived at Etwell House, they say he used to walk the nine miles from Andover to exercise hounds, and then walk back.[16] This was an example of his keenness and tough physical condition, also perhaps the time taken, was a reason why he moved to Fyfield, a house only half the distance from his beloved pack.

In 1899 summer tents were packed away from the First Practice Camp, and trains of General Service waggons pulled by heavy horses were seen to trundle slowly along the old coachroad from Salisbury to Marlborough. The road follows Nine Mile River first on its south bank, and then it crosses to wind across Milston and Brigmerston downs, towards the Swindon, Marlborough and Andover Railway.[17] Columns of soldiers, regulars and volunteers alike, marched through the early morning mist, dust and damp towards their return to barrack-squares or drill-halls for winter drill. Then cub-hunting could begin in earnest.

The new Master was a pleasant chap, with great sense of duty. He was a big man with a moustache, and perhaps he was short-sighted as later pictures show him wearing a monocle. Enthusiastic and passionately fond of hunting, he spared no money or energy to keep the country in good shape, never asking for any subscription. Strangely no newspaper reports have survived, and it appears that any diaries he kept during the entire years of his mastership are not in existence. However, Kathleen Philip tells us a great deal about his forceful character and talent for getting things done, in her book *Gigha. The Flourishing Island.*

The family were no absentee landlords. Gigha was home. They spent the summer on the island returning to Fyfield for cub-hunting. He was also a great believer in co-operation with his staff so that Fred Perrin and J. Goater remained to whip-in and preserve the continuity of hunt tradition. They proved excellent Hunt servants with a thorough knowledge of the country.[18] The New Forest portion was again given up to the Hursley, and Wherwell Wood, that elegantly beautiful series of coverts on the Test, was once more relinquished to foxes and fishermen.

We do not know what type of hunter he favoured although William Watt Philip, his factor on Gigha, took a keen interest in Clydesdale horses.[19] Later photographs show Yorke Scarlett, by then an almost majestic figure, although heavy, but still energetic, riding this type of thoroughbred cross.[20]

He appears to have been dissatisfied with the pack he bought on Mr. Shrubb's demise, perhaps due to the Master's illness, nobody had attended to careful breeding. During Scarlett's time at the helm the type of hound he bred from was revolutionised. It seems he favoured hounds of a light and racy type, and we know he liked to hunt downs and woodland. Otherwise a powerful, heavier-looking hound would have been needed for plough, or marshy ground, and to jump ditches. We must not forget that the Vale was much wetter than it is today.

However, of pressing concern to our story are the remarkable changes taking place in the country as a whole. Victoria, Queen of Great Britain, Ireland and Empress of India together with one-third of the globe, died on 22 January 1901. Her reign saw the zenith of British Imperial power built on the entrepreneurial talent of persons such as Assheton Smith. Henry James wrote:

"We all feel a bit motherless now. Mysterious little Victoria is dead and fat, vulgar Edward is King".

For the coronation celebrations of Edward VII at Amesbury, Sir Edmund and Lady Antrobus, still enthusiastic members of the Hunt, gave a dinner of roast beef, plum-pudding and powerful home-brew to five hundred labourers and their families. This was similar to the repast given at the Diamond Jubilee of Victoria.[21]

By 1903 irrevocable change had come to Tidworth. Tedworth House was now the military quarter for the General Officer Commanding Salisbury Plain, and later the G.O.C. in C. Southern Command.[22] Let us look through Yorke Scarlett's eyes as he might have led hounds from kennels to a traditional meeting place at Hougoumont farm. He would have kept to the high ground. Below, an army of workmen from the corrugated tin shacks at Ludgershall, known as 'Tin Town' or 'Navvy Village', were erecting the giant barracks of Aliwal, Assaye, Candahar and Mooltan.[23] Clarendon Hill gave the Master a clear view of Tidworth railway station[24] opened in 1902, where uncovered waggons brought men, coal, timber, bricks and steel for the great new military centre, and meat, bread, milk, tea and beer for the men.

Traversing Clarendon Hill hounds were understandably interested in the gorgeous smell coming from the sewage works, while crossing the Pennings, foxes, hares and pheasants fled to the sanctuary of Sidbury Hill frightened by fencing and ditching operations in the fresh military cemetery being prepared for the service dead.

During a smart canter across Cow Down towards Hougoumont the Master's keen eye would have noted the Midland and South Western Union Railway[25] line cutting the country, and impeding fast hunting from the Bourne river to Collingbourne Wood. He might have shaken his head sadly, even though train drivers were ordered to give a warning whistle to horses and hounds. Empty trucks on this line carried stable manure to Hampshire strawberries, and hound or cur dog droppings to tanneries in the Midlands.

Brigadier-General Hope writing of Yorke Scarlett tells us that in his time a good scent usually hung on the downs and in Pewsey Vale, and there was not a great deal of ploughed land.

He goes on that:

"Among many enjoyable hunts one of the best was from Everleigh Ashes after a poor morning."

Did the Master, we wonder, ride his hack the many miles to the Ashes from Fyfield!

"The hounds found in the late afternoon in winter, with frost coming on," the report goes on. "They ran at top pace over Sidbury Hill, by Netheravon, crossed the River Avon and killed on Ell Barrow, without a check or being handled in any way. Horses could not keep up with hounds and only two or three of the whole field were up, beside the Master and hunt servants. That good sportsman Mr. Tom Baily of Thruxton was one of the fortunate survivors".

Black Heath to the west of Ell Barrow appeared indigo, as glimpsed through warm vapour rising from steaming hounds and the broken fox. The shallow, narrow valleys of Salisbury Plain appeared to heave, its troughs elevated, and the crests sinking as in a restless ocean.

Yorke Scarlett dismounted from a beaten horse. Walking along the Ditch towards Lavington Folly, his feet crunched frozen thistles sporting prickles like steel barbs. And his heavy boots crumbled ant-runs resembling burnt pastry. In frost and half-darkness the descent to Netheravon was hazardous, the Avon river being petrified with icicles, with stiffening grass on dead bullrush banks. Lights from The Old Brewery beckoned through the darkness, until sudden mist enveloped Figheldean Fields.

Arthur Hussey's hospitality was famous. Hounds were found loose-boxes, porridge and a supply of bones. Harriers in kennel were furious! The two Masters, hot whisky in hand, talked hunting by a beechwood fire, which spat sparks onto a stone hearth. The scent of roast pheasant, braising lamb and apple pie made Yorke Scarlett realise it was ten hours since breakfast-time.

In the dining-room taking pride of place on the sideboard, a silver cup was displayed. Arthur picked it up, happy, his eyes smiling with pleasure. The cup was two-handled, about ten and a half inches in height and decorated with leaves and flowers. An inscription reads:

A. HUSSEY MASTER OF HARRIERS

and on the reverse

PRESENTED BY THE OFFICERS ROYAL ARTILLERY, BULFORD MAY 1903.

This interesting gift is alive and well and still lives at Larkhill! The cup is of special significance because Arthur, growing up near the bright sparkle of Avon and Bourne rivers found that otterhunting became his great love. He was amateur huntsman in 1900 to Mr. Courtenay Tracey's Otterhounds, and these hounds were kennelled at Holywell in Hampshire on the Meon river. Thus Hussey must have been grateful for the help and co-operation of army officers, in caring for the two packs. A photograph of 1906 shows him with hounds and flanked by three whippers-in, one of whom is probably "Taffy" Walwyn.

By 1907 this generous young Master donated his harehounds as a gift to the artillery officers of Bulford, and Netheravon hounds became the Royal Artillery (Bulford) Harriers.[26]

This was the advent of two packs hunting the Salisbury Plain Training area.

With Bulford garrison in mind, we might follow Yorke Scarlett making his way back to Tedworth kennels the following morning. A frost wind would have made him take the coachroad which follows the Avon valley. Foxes can always be found in the withy beds, clustering in alternate crescents, between Upavon and Bulford. But a huntsman has to work on foot. Reed-beds are deep, and horses flounder.

Passing the line of beeches beyond Figheldean, Syrencot House glared sulkily through the trees, angry at its owner being forced to sell his estate to the Army. Opposite St. Leonard's church, Bulford, stands Mr. Ledger Hill's manorhouse, another casualty of compulsory purchase and today the permanent quarter of the Commander in Chief U.K. Land Forces.

At the garrison, the timber and tin hutted camp had increased in size. There were six lines of barracks, offices and guardrooms,[27] although the hundreds of white bell-tents, looking like upturned lilies, would not be pitched in the grassy, well-drained valley until the summer. Contractors had already started three brick riding-schools, as half-man, half-horse, the British army campaigned on its tens of thousands of horses. And all officers were instructed in equitation.

Returning to our Master, 30 March 1905 was a joyful day when a son was born to his wife Mabel. She was the daughter of Colonel the Hon. Algernon Annesley.[28]

On Gigha, the solid wooden pier thrusting out into deep water and built

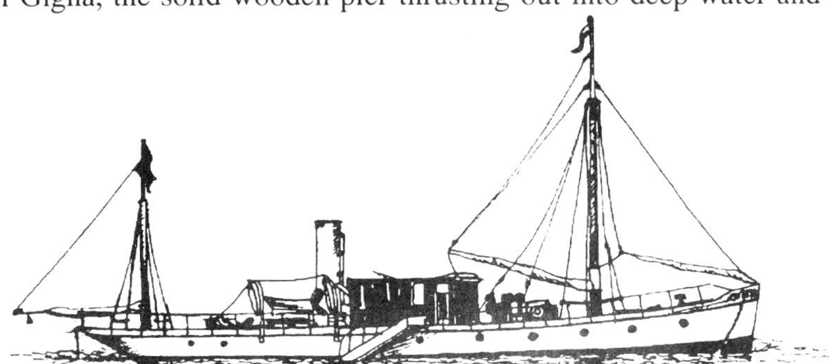

Alias "Snapshot".
The steam yacht is of similar dimensions and design to "Snapshot" built by T. B. Seath at Rutherglen in 1895.

by the Laird in 1895 must have been crowded. Tenants would have decorated the landing-stage with coloured bunting and raised a cheer to welcome the family and new heir for the summer, when the Scarlett's steam yacht "Snapshot" berthed on the island. The family lived for long periods at their true home lovely Achamore House, with its full staff, handsome furniture, oil lamps and hip baths. The mansion is set in sixty acres of gardens and parkland, with its own island golf course and Home Farm. Many guests sailed for weekends and parties, or the famous agricultural show, enlivened by the Kilberry pipers,[29] all brought from the mainland by the energy of William Yorke Scarlett together with "Snapshot".

Brigadier-General Hope says that the Duke of Beaufort twice visited Savernake Forest. On the first occasion sport was bad and foxes in short supply, but the second time the Duke had a very good hunt finishing well into the Craven country. Woodland hunting was Yorke Scarlett's great love. Even at this early date he may have been planning to breed a special type of hound based on Welsh blood for this work.

The 1905-6 season was his last with the Tedworth. Recalling that he was previously Master of the Craven and followed Major Gerald Ricardo, who bred the best pack the Craven ever had, it was understandable that he brought the previous breeding policy up to date, concentrating on the smaller mettlesome Belvoir sort.[30] His great-nephew tells us that he never put a hound in the pack, unless he had hunted its forebears.

Reading the *Foxhound Kennel Studbook* we see that only Tedworth Rubicon '94 on Wallflower '95 were bred from; together with a litter from Tedworth Tyrant '97 out of Ringlet '94. Entered puppies were from the Bicester, Belvoir and Warwickshire kennels; while Scottish packs were also favoured, the Lanark & Renfrew, Mr. A. MacKenzie's and the Duke of Buccleuch's whose blood was of the Belvoir - Grafton - Brocklesby - Pychley or Warwickshire sorts.

1901 shows the same trend. Only Tyrant together with Valesman '97 and Watchman '98 on Tedworth bitches were used. All other puppies were of the Belvoir type. As *The Huntsman's Log Book* says:

"The vogue for Belvoir in the years (1900 et seq) was so great that their drafts, whether young or old, were avidly sought after often being booked years ahead."

Also "Although there were more stallion hounds at Belvoir than in any other kennel at the time, so great became the call on them that it was becoming impossible to cope with the demand."

Breeding up to 1906 gives a similar pattern, and in 1905 the Duke of Beaufort's famous Diver '01 and brother Discount, hounds of sterling quality, were used to enhance the Tedworth. It is noted that forty brace of foxes was the average accounted for in each season with forty-five being the best tally.

In May 1906 Yorke Scarlett resigned his mastership to return to the Craven where he took the helm for a further thirteen years. However, this deeply favourite Master was a close associate with our Hunt for over fifty years until after World War II. His Tedworth friends presented him with a silver rosebowl.

Chapter 5

Sir Edmund Antrobus and the Hunt Committee 1906 - 1915

Stonehenge

Days of extravagant grandeur for Britain and her Empire, elegantly reflected in the hunting field, were drawing to a close. Roads were being built to hurry *matériels* of war over the Plain and link Tidworth with Bulford. Also a Tilshead to Shrewton metalled road was laid,[1] so that ponies in traps, dog-carts and Broughams no longer braved volunteers' stray bullets. Three years later, a War Department locomotive worked by Royal Engineers pulled freight waggons along the railway line linking Amesbury with Larkhill.

1906 was the summer solstice when Sir Edmund Antrobus, the esteemed Chairman of the Hunt Committee, allowed himself to be blindfolded and initiated into the Most Ancient Order of Druids. What would his father and grandfather have said! The initiation of Sir Edmund was a feather in the Druids' white headpieces, because five years earlier he had insisted they pay a shilling each whenever they visited Stonehenge.[2] The present plans for Stonehenge are estimated to cost sixteen million pounds. History amusing itself?

Saying farewell to Mr. Yorke Scarlett the Tedworth Hunt had to find a new Master, and a series of masterships followed with no fewer than thirteen changes during the next twenty-one years. This inevitably altered the character of the Hunt, with the Committee playing a more dominant role. The Age of the Hunt Committee had arrived because Yorke Scarlett was the last Master to hunt almost entirely at his own expense.

The 1906-07 season saw Mr. John Edward Arthur Willis Fleming of Stoneham Park and Chilworth take over for one year only. Born and bred a Hampshireman he was the son of John Brown Willis Fleming, a famous yachtsman. The new Master was educated at Eton and Pembroke College, Oxford.[3]

As a boy he was devoted to the chase. At fifteen, like Assheton Smith and Yorke Scarlett before him, he hunted beagles near the family seat. But the pack was too slow for horses so he turned to harriers. Hares were the quarry and even deer. In 1906, wire and shooting, the scourge of hunting made him give up the pack.[4] It was our good fortune that Willis Fleming came to Tedworth.

An engraving shows a tall, slim young man, very smart and wearing the old-fashioned long hunting coat with five buttons. It seems that Mrs. Fleming was as fanatic a hunting woman as her husband, and brought up sons and daughters as avid foxhunters.[5]

Always well-mounted, Bugleman, Nell Gwynne, Killarney Boy and Peter carried the sporting family to hunt the excellent hounds. The F.K.S.B. 1908 shows the breeding policy continuing as previously with the Duke of Beaufort's Druid '04, by the famous Diver '01, again figuring.[6]

The 1907-08 season saw Major Henry Connop of Ramridge succeed as Master once again for one year only. He lived at Fyfield House because Yorke Scarlett was hunting the Craven. After leaving Sherborne School there was no grand tour of Europe for him; the classical tour designed to make dull boys into gentlemen of taste. Connop travelled and shot bear in the Rocky Mountains, and antelope or lion in South Africa. Also he rode in the first steeplechase meeting held in Bulawayo. His photograph shows a suave young man in bush kit, with mounted cane, and wearing leather gaiters and boots of brilliant polish.[7]

In England our hero hunted with Lord Portsmouth's pack, then with the Cheshire and Meynell. He also had occasional days with the Blackmore Vale and Hambledon, hunting stag on Exmoor and the New Forest. Between times he rode in the Crawley and Horsham point-to-points for Mr. G. H. Courage; and did his loyal duty as Captain in the Imperial Yeomanry. Perhaps as a counter-balance his Honorary Hunt Secretary, Mr. John Draper Best, commenced hunting with the Tedworth at an early age and remained faithful to our pack. Fred Perrin, who came with the Shrubbs, hunted hounds for Mr. Connop to retain continuity. The F.K.S.B. says that breeding policy remained unaltered.

For over eighty years two black leather bound books, one backed in red morocco, have stood patiently on library shelves, or lain despondently in drawers awaiting resurrection. These are the Tedworth Hunt Minute Books 1909-29 and 28 February 1912 to 16 June 1937. A Committee, often chaired by three generations of the Antrobus family (with or without Druids), has been in existence since Mr. Assheton Smith's death in 1858, but these are the earliest written records extant today.

The cover of the 1909-29 book bears a label saying "Western Division Minute Book". And readers must be no more surprised to find that Tedworth country had been divided into two parts than was the President of the Committee, Henry fifth Marquess of Ailesbury!

"Venator", who hunted with the Tedworth in the 1870's and writing in the *Marlborough Times and Wilts and Berks County* newspaper of 2 May 1908, feels that the Marquess had been treated with scant courtesy by the Hunt Committee. It seems that he knew nothing about the proposed division until everything was as good as settled.

The Marquess, who succeeded to the title in 1894, always gave the best of all support to the Hunt, and we are sure knowing the type of man he was, that Ailesbury considered the new proposals with logic and care.

Guided by his grandson and biographer, who wrote an excellent book *The Wardens of Savernake Forest* we can picture Henry Brudenell-Bruce,

Marquess of Ailesbury 1894-1911 driving an open carriage through his beloved forest. The carriage horses were elderly but full of spirit. They matched the tall, burly distinguished Marquess with his full-bearded, intelligent face, always surmounted by a hat or smoking-cap to conceal his bald pate. Plagued with deafness, the impediment had impeded advancement when he sat as Member of Parliament for Chippenham.

The Marquess had inherited appalling debts from previous generations, together with lost assets squandered by the "Black Sheep", who maybe is remembered for his canary yellow coat, babbling staghounds and champagne. However, that day the Marquess might have appeared thoughtful. Normally he never tired of driving around Savernake admiring old trees, approving new planting, or supervising carefully the upkeep of roads and cottages. He was thinking over the letter the Hunt Secretary had written asking for his blessing on the division of the country into Eastern and Western sides, an action already decided upon. The old Marquess pondered. Division spoke of fragmentation, a course that from bitter experience he adamantly disapproved of.

Still there might be no help for it. Times were changing. Therefore with reluctance he decided to agree and impose conditions. Firstly the whole of Savernake estate should be in Western Division. Two packs must never hunt his land. And secondly, should a new Master be found willing to hunt the country as a whole, then the dual committee must merge into one.

The President's decision would have been uppermost in their minds when the Committee met at the Phoenix Hotel, Pewsey, on 6 April 1908. Sir Edmund Antrobus took the chair, when it was decided to advertise for a new Master in the *Horse and Hound.* At the next meeting on the 20th, Hugh de H. Whatton of Rockley, the Treasurer, proposed that Arthur Hussey take over the dog pack from May 1st. His acceptance was warmly applauded as members knew he was already heavily engaged in hunting the Courtenay Tracey Otterhounds during summer months. Major Geddes, Master of the Royal Artillery (Bulford) Harriers, and himself a working Committee member, undoubtedly offered to help.

1907-08 was Fred Perrin's last season and about this time he left hunt service to take up the tenancy of the military Manor Farm at Shipton Bellinger.[8] His son Charlie, aged fourteen, whipped-in to Fred and remembers one of Perrin's last hunts. From Tedworth kennels, Dunch Hill, now the Tidworth Golf Course, constructed in 1905, held no foxes. Nor did Nine Mile valley and even the Plain was blank.

Returning after a disappointing day, Bulford Gorses provided a bold dog fox. Off screamed the pack, and on they went to Everleigh in approaching dark. Pressing Charlie past Everleigh Ashes the pack raced down the hill without a check, horses following only by the killing cry. Nobody knows how the fox, hounds, huntsman and whipper-in crossed at Burbage Wharf, but Charlie Perrin swears their pilot was accounted for at two a.m. in Savernake forest![9]

Fortune came in the shape of cheerful Walter Vavasour Faber, formerly Captain in the Royal Horse Artillery, he was later Lieutenant Colonel Commanding Royal Wiltshire Imperial Yeomanry. A talented horseman of powerful physique, the colonel was a partner in Strong & Co, brewers of Romsey, and Member of Parliament for Andover. Work in the House being less than onerous, he stayed Master 1908-11.[10] Tom Astley, who came from the Rufford, was appointed huntsman.[11]

"Another Grand Run with the Tedworth Hounds," exulted a news article in January 1909, giving over eight column inches and a sketch map from start to finish. The point was a brilliant sixteen miles in two hours thirty-eight minutes.

"This hunt," said Captain Faber, "maybe and will be called 'Tom Astley's hunt'. And the man who helped him, when help became necessary, was his whipper-in Harry Grange."

Symes, Lord Ailesbury's keeper, had a fox in a tree not two hundred yards from the meet at Puthall Gate when hounds dislodged him at eleven-eighteen. A beautiful long-legged fox he was, and dark in colour. Hounds started close to pug, scenting up the wild west wind at a very fair pace. The forest shivered with excitement, branches grabbing at ladies' busvines. Across the soft grass of the Ruins sped Charlie and along the road maintained at Lord Ailesbury's expense to the Column. Tottenham House stood empty and alone, Ailesbury having to live at Leigh Hill to save money. Past Durley our pilot crossed the Kennet and Avon canal at the bridge, rather than soaking his brush in cluttered weed.

At the station, the guard was shouting to railway passengers:

"Savernake . . . . . Savernake. Change for Marlborough. Next stop Pewsey . . . . ." as Mr. Osmond, our old friend the butcher's grandson in black coat and bereft of meat-basket, bent through luggage trolleys on his cob. Because this is a friendly hunt, noblemen, gentry, farmers, tradesmen and all everyday folk met as equals. A brace of Reverends gave Great Western Railway passengers a wide berth lest they were C. of E. congregation. And three ladies vied with sportsmen to jump the fence.

On went the fox at a steady pace. Confident, never rushing. Burbage, Easton, Milton Lilbourne, Pewsey, a Bradshaw railway timetable guide would have come in handy for any visitor to the Hunt. At Wilcot the Master, a modest man, took a hand. In Astley's absence he cast hounds over the road and through a herd of cattle. Left handed to Woodborough then Alton, with a check at All Cannings, where Astley had to wade the water, Captain Faber never told how he and Mr. Maurice jumped the bridge arch, to go on alone with hounds, because he gave the glory to Astley.

At Patney station they beat the train, and finally gave that stout fox best in the Duke of Beaufort's country. Every hound save one was up, a tribute to Yorke Scarlett breeding.

Returning to our Minute Book we see that on 10 April 1910 the cost of forage was perhaps more than a good thing! The Poultry Fund had been settled to the greatest advantage possible, both to the satisfaction of the Hunt and the people who made claims. Luckily the Treasurer had enough money to pay which was a saving grace! A guarantee of five hundred pounds was voted for Western Division.

Thanks were recorded to the Secretary who had written over a hundred letters. Present day subscribers please note because Secretaries have ten times the workload! Also thanks to Colonel Geddes, posted abroad on promotion for his help in looking after the military area. Captain Popham, the new Master R.A. (Bulford) Hunt, was elected to the Committee as he was a very good Wiltshireham!

The 10 May saw the death of fashionable Edward VII, architect of the Anglo-French Entente Cordiale, and an Anglo-Russian Alliance. However, storm clouds were brewing with the German Emperor, and Edward personally supported the great military reforms of Lord Haldane, Secretary of State for War.[12]

Salisbury Plain had to be provisioned with guns, ammunition, soldiers, waggons and horses, with twenty-one camps. Today Windmill Hill, Fargo Down and Pond Farm camps are no more than long lost memories.

In contrast, hunting a drag is indeed a heinous thing! That is if it is malicious! And the meeting on 28 December 1910 exploded. Minutes recorded:

"That we express most strongly our fullest confidence in our most worthy and excellent Master Captain Faber . . . . . and call upon those who have publicly stated that the Tedworth hunts drags, to prove their statement or withdraw it.

(Signed) Hugh de H. Whatton"

Intriguingly, his accusers turned out to be astonishingly Colonel Harmar and Mr. G. Young, of Huish, both Members of the Hunt Committee. Their letters were read at 11 January meeting 1911, together with Captain Faber's oblique and precipitous resignation. In the best interests of the Hunt, Harmar withdrew his contentious letter, while Young said that:

"He had written in chaff!"

Confused, the Committee hardly knew what to think. They could only guess and put a brave face on it.

Troubles like this come in couples. The *Wiltshire Gazette* on 8 June 1911 had a field-day. It hinted that Faber's abrupt decision to resign might be linked to unsigned letters and disagreeable telegrams regarding discrepancies in Hunt accounts. The newspaper devoted over four feet of column space to titillate eager readers hungry for scandal. Headlines asserted:

"THE FUTURE OF THE TEDWORTH

Meetings at Pewsey and Andover

EACH SIDE SUPPORTS THE COMMITTEE

The New Master"

The *Gazette* was reporting the Pewsey meeting at the Phoenix Hotel. River Street. Attendance was disappointingly low, because maybe people did not want to be involved with scandal. In the E-shaped function room, Sir Edmund Antrobus was ensconced with his back to the garden window, while a row of farmers sitting at the street end puffed on their pipes, took snuff and looked at Sir Edmund expectantly. Arthur Hussey, seated near one of the black marble fireplaces, commented to G. W. Young:

"The evergreen situation of the mastership!" while a lady in a lawn dress and straw hat thought Mr. Hayward looked worried.

Sir Edmund spoke:

"As a rule when a Master resigns a meeting is called to accept his resignation, or otherwise."

Someone said "Shame!" amidst muttering at the back.

"Good chap!" agreed a snuff-taker.

"In April Captain Faber was extremely ill."

"He's gone to Harrogate, or so they say," whispered Straw Hat to her companion in a blue silk cravat.

"Quiet please!" Then after a pause, "The decision of your Committee needs some explanation, because we were forced to terminate Hunt staff's engagements, and advertise for a new Master."

"He resigned in April. 'Tis June now."

"What about the letters?" objected a dissenter.

"Not signed were they?"

"Let's have some facts."

"The telegrams were the trouble", sighed Blue Cravat. "The whole town knows. Bad business."

"Order please. First, I will read Captain Faber's letter."

A stout subscriber went downstairs for half a pint of port. Sir Edmund's voice droned on and on and no-one seemed to listen, each having his private opinion.

". . . . . unable to continue the mastership . . . . . management of the Hunt . . . . . not free to attend to private affairs . . . . . health given me trouble lately . . . . . pleasure to me to look back on mastership . . . . ."

Straw Hat lady looked in the mahogany mirror with its handsome pediment, and wondered if her face was peeling after driving to Devizes Wool Sale in the sun. Her companion stretched restlessly against the black oak settle because the sharp carving of a grinning cat's head was hurting his back.

"Regarding the reasons given for Captain Faber's resignation," went on Sir Edmund, raising his voice to control the meeting, "We are sorry to say that there was a difference of opinion in the Hunt."

"You were one of them weren't you Arthur?" said Young.

"And you do not differ from the Committee, I hope Mr. Hussey?" snapped the Chairman.

"Not much. No."

"I hope not at all." After a pause, "Let us get on. Letters were written to the papers. A Bruce Lamb wrote . . . . ."

"Oh! Ah!" grumbled a tobacco pipe, sucking hard.

" . . . . . his letter was received by Admiral Marx, Secretary to our Andover side of the country."

The letter was long, the June evening warm, and people wanted to get on with it. They were curious to learn about the new Master. However, they pricked up their ears on hearing.

"I am at a loss," writes Lamb, "to understand the item of tradesmen's accounts, as audited being £1,746* is arrived at. With a terrific outstanding liability of £447. These outstanding liabilities are *not shown in the published accounts of the Hunt.*"

**At 1993 prices about £70,000.*

Knowing his audience Sir Edmund called a recess for refreshment and lobbying in the bar. Later order was restored and the proposed vote of confidence in the Committee was unanimous. Everyone cheered up when the nomination of Captain Malet as the new Master was discussed.

Young Captain Malet was very keen. Formerly of the 8th Hussars he lived at Wilbury Park,[13] the home of our late lamented Master the Hon. Percy Scawen Wyndham. The Chairman stressed that Malet was a Wiltshireman who belonged to an old county family. He was very willing to take the country for a guarantee of £1,500 for three days a week, and fortunately did not wish to hunt hounds himself. This meant that Ashley, our excellent kennel huntsman who succeeded Fred Perrin, could continue hunting hounds. Otherwise we might have lost him to another pack.

Meantime at Ludgershall the Hunt meeting at the Prince of Wales Hotel had to be postponed. Troops were coming to the Plain. Germany was re-arming, and the Hotel was commandeered.

Hound breeding during these years was interesting. The Hunt had seventy couple in kennels. It was hoped to sell twenty couples at profit, because drafts from Lord Portman's splendid pack had been bought for £158. The F.K.S.B. says that Belvoir drafts, including progeny from the famous Warlaby '04 were obtained, also drafts from Lord Bathurst's (the V.W.H.).

We wish records had told us which gentleman was in charge of breeding policy. With such a turnover of Masters, the pack might easily have become a shambles. Blessed indeed are those countries where a family pack descends from father to son, because it often takes years for a Master to find out which blood lines suits his country best and start breeding to a particular type.

Overall policy might have been in the hands of Mr. Henry Sutton, a son of Sir Richard, or perhaps Captain F. C. Sutton of Penton is a likely candidate, as is Mr. W. H. Fowle of Chute Lodge. It is these families, with the hereditary Marquess of Ailesbury as President, that provided the rigid skeleton to the Hunt.

Captain Malet stayed for one year only and on 27 March 1912 the general meeting received the ebullient Irishman, Mr. Oswald C. H. Riley, with applause. He lived in the huntsman's cottage at Tedworth House,[14] as it seems he had little money and was unable to bear the expense of keeping his own horses. Unlike Captain Malet he hunted hounds himself for four days a week. Riley proved an explosive sportsman, and very keen about hounds.

On March 12 1914 headlines in the *Standard* screamed:

"THE DRAG-LAYER

VIGOROUS PROTEST BY THE TEDWORTH

HUNT

THRASHING INCIDENT

"The remarkable incident which occurred recently in the hunting field, when the Master of the Tedworth Hunt, Mr. Oswald Riley, thrashed a horseman, whom he overtook and accused of drag-laying came under review at a special meeting chaired by Sir Edmund Antrobus, those present included Lord Grantley, Mr. F. R. Sutton, Admiral Marx, Colonel Harmar,

Captain Malet, Mr. W. H. Fowle and Mr. Hugh de Heinz Whatton.

Sir Edmund, in the hot seat as usual, said:

"Mr. Riley had no right to take the matter into his own hands, but he was keen about hounds. And keen to show sport. When he saw somebody interfering in this unsportsmanlike manner, it was a very trying thing for him to keep his (Irish) temper!"

Either there was someone with a grudge or there were "antis" about! It should be realised that there have always been virulent anti-hunting protesters. The man who was thrashed seems to have been working on orders from a shadowy group. Perhaps he demanded 'danger money', because no charges seem to have been brought.

This was the official line. But an extraordinary entry in the Minute Book says:

"Letters from I. Berry stating he had been accused of the connivance. He denied doing anything *without the approval of the Master.*" These letters were kept secret and never divulged to the public.

As before so many times, a new Master had to be appointed. Although in fairness to Riley it seems that cash was the cause of his resignation. He could not afford to hunt hounds. And the Committee was unable to offer more guarantee money.

The new Master, Mr. H. W. Boileau, a light-weight rider and relation of Ethyl Boileau the novelist, could be assured of calming the situation. He had hunted beagles in 1878, later he hunted the Wirrall (Cheshire) Harriers, the South Coast Staghounds, the Old Surrey and was present Master of the South Berkshire.[15] Age and experience are necessary in difficult times.

Two months later on 28 June 1914 the Archduke Francis Ferdinand and his wife were shot in the streets of Sarajevo by a Bosnian fanatic.

Great Britain declared war on 4 August 1914.[16]

Could hounds be kept or no? This was the question the 14 October meeting had to resolve. Army officers' subscriptions were no longer taken, and Admiral Marx was on active service. A letter from Major Thompson, of the Army Remount Depot, Winchester, asked gentlemen to take in, handle and keep fit a number of Canadian horses at say 15s to £1 a week. Fifty thousand Canadians were coming.

With the Canadians came the rain. Bulford Manor flooded. Shrewton was under four feet of water. Overcrowded in huts and canvas cities, Bulford, Larkhill and Tidworth camps had trench feet and dysentery. Transport broke down and food was short at Bustard, Westdown North and South as well as the notorious Pond Farm, while horses starved when fodder failed to arrive. Soldiers lie under pathetic little mounds in graveyards of Bulford and Netheravon.[17]

Then snow fell. In white stillness hunting was restricted to Savernake and Collingbourne, the sixth Marquess of Ailesbury accepted half-rent.

On 28 October 1914 Mr. Fowle walked slowly to the Chairman's table at the Prince of Wales Hotel. He remained standing. The Committee stood with bowed heads.

"Sir Edmund," said Mr. Fowle, "will not be attending tonight. He has received a telegram saying his only child and heir was killed at Ypres on the

24th." He paused in the closed silence.

"My wife and I received a telegram this afternoon. Our only son and heir was killed on the same day. Also was the son of our late Chairman, the Duke of Wellington."

At a dug-out above the British dressing-station, Lieutenant Colonel J. M. McRae, of the Royal Canadian Medical Corps. wrote:

"In Flanders Fields the Poppies Grow."

On 7 April 1915 Sir Edmund Antrobus died of a broken heart.

Chapter 6

War and Peace 1915 - 1925

9.2 inch Howitzer. Laid at the highest angle of elevation.
(From "The Story of the Gun", A. W. Wilson.)

On the whole, things turned out better than expected. That spring, Chandos, Marquess of Ailesbury became Chairman of the Hunt with Mr. W. H. Fowle as President. Military subscribers came forward in a most generous way, their only request being that hounds met each Saturday within ten miles of Bulford at one o'clock. Mr. Boileau agreed to go on hunting as long as he had any horses left. The army were commandeering everything that walked for chargers, gun-teams and limbers.

However by May 1915 Mr. Boileau resigned, and Lord Ailesbury, wearing a Major's uniform, welcomed our old friend Mr. Yorke Scarlett at the May meeting. He was to hunt twice a week. The Committee would keep hounds, taking them to meets, and provide hunt servants' horses, as long as finances (and remount officers) permitted.

Yorke Scarlett passionately loved the chase, and hunting woodland was his delight. In an expertly maintained forest, leaves from ancient oak, and straight well-grown beech litter the forest floor in a rich mass. Voices and hunting horn notes echo and re-echo. Words, music and thoughts pass from tree to tree on the æther. A network of overhead branches form sombre aisles beneath winter cloud, and voices laughingly repeat:

"Eleu in there my lads!
Eu in there, little bitches!

Leu in."

One keen December morning, we believe the Master became a very disturbed man. Most probably hunting hounds himself, with Astley, an expert in woodland venery, whipping-in, hounds might have been hunting slowly from Tangley towards Doles Wood. The forest was a favourite haunt of both foxes and huntsmen. Let us take some snapshots of the devastation the war brought to hunting people.

War Office orders had already reduced the pack from a normal fifty to twenty-five couples. Biplanes from 4 Squadron the Royal Flying Corps at Netheravon were probably enacting a dogfight overhead![1] As Yorke Scarlett entered Blagdon Wood, despatch riders with brand new motor bicycles[2] practised jumping over ditches and avoiding trees, for service amidst barbed-wire and trenches of the Western Front. Hounds lost their fox, noses filled with petrol fume and distant smoke.

He rode on, speaking to hounds softly.

"Y-ert . . . . . y-ert . . . . . y-ert . . . . ."

Branches a mile away sighed as axes brought oaks, ash and beech crashing to the forest floor, and made horses' ears prick, their flanks shiver. Further on, the ground grew white and hot from stick fires, while huntsman and pack stood their ground at the edge of a stripped clearing.

Before them was empty space. A swathe of Doles Wood had been clean-felled for ammunition boxes, pit-props and duckboards. Huts at Bulford if placed end to end would have made a wood building six miles long.

To the south the land falls sharply to Devil's Ditch. The felled forest exposed billions of flints, to tear out bearings of engines, and horseshoe clenches. The sky above distant hills was lemon shading to dove-grey. A fringe of men, some working, some taking a dinner of bread and cheese, washed down with cold tea from *"Corona"* bottles, were hacking their way towards the Andover road. A few venerable oaks were left standing. Heaven knows why. Perhaps the trees wept, or were spared for luck. Down the road leading to Andover station, lines of timber-waggons, drawn by teams of six or eight horses, pulled away to steam trains and chaos.

Today the Forest District Manager writes that West Woods, South Grove and Collingbourne were also creamed-off in the First World War. The crop was what is called coppice with standards, that is, hazel coppice with a smattering of big mature oak trees. The Forestry Commission started replanting West Woods and Collingbourne in 1933. The remaining areas were re-stocked between 1946 and 1960.[3]

Mr. Fowle, taking the chair at the August 1917 meeting, said that due to petrol rationing the Master, with great reluctance, was unable to hunt the Tedworth again although he continued to be joint Master of the Craven until 1919. However, we need not say goodbye to Willie Yorke Scarlett yet. He will soon be back for another thirty year stint.

At least he was more fortunate than his friend Arthur Hussey, now Lieutenant in the mounted Wiltshire Regiment[4] As cavalry were outdated in trench warfare, except for running messages, he was never posted to France, and became Master of both the Royal Artillery (Bulford) Harriers as well as the Courtenay Tracey Otterhounds. Due to the menace of German U-boats in 1917, lack of food forced Captain Hussey to put down his beloved pack of harriers.[5]

Foxhounds continued to protect chickens and baby lambs from foxes. Eating well on swill from Tidworth Garrison, the sterling Tom Astley hunted hounds. Mr. C. G. G. Hilton Green, later joint Master of the Old Berkshire, and Captain W. H. Alexander of Upavon, nicknamed "Tiny" being six feet four inches in height, whipped-in.[6] Brigadier General Hope tells us:

"Captain Alexander . . . . . was full of good stories and well-known to all hunting folk over a large area. When too heavy to ride he founded the Pewsey Vale beagles, a beautiful little pack of fourteen and a half inch hounds, which he afterwards gave to Lord Melchett, who later hunted the Tedworth, to amuse his boys and train them up in the way they should go."[7]

But with no Master, difficulties arose, and officers of Tidworth garrison galloped to the rescue, whom the Sub-Commandant authorised to carry on hunting. As well as General Lumby and Colonel Harman, five other officers including Captain Kingscote were voted on the Committee, to hunt hounds two days a week. Having Army help was fortunate. Even in 1918 hunt servants had to have military passes to ride, because spy stories and Bolshevik scares were everywhere.

The 1918-19 season brought Captain Maurice John Kingscote, formerly of the Bucks Yeomanry, as Master. He lived at Pinkney Court, Malmesbury, and his father was Gentleman of the Cellar and Gentleman Usher in Ordinary to King George V. Later Maurice was a talented Master of the V.W.H. and the Meynell in 1940.[8]

Perhaps we might follow Captain Kingscote as he left Tedworth House Officers' Club to walk slowly across the park in the direction of kennels. Three years previously in 1915, the mansion had been made into a Club, with a subscription of 2/-s (10p) per officer. Facilities included golf and games generally.[9]

On this August day 1918 the grass was parched. Only the Plantation green and glass-still, enfolding the Mausoleum built by Assheton Smith, offered solace, even though he and Matilda lie sleeping in the little Burial Chapel in Church Lane. Kingscote must have thought it a pity, that when the Mausoleum was built, the Master's old kennels were demolished, because replacement kennels were falling down.

Ahead of him lay the narrow road leading to Home Farm, and he could see the Sanitary Officer's dogcart awaiting him. Even at that distance the smell from kennels was appalling! Something had to be done.

Braving the stench, the two men walked past the farmhouse to a brick building lying at right angles to it. Today the whitewashed building has sightless windows and crouches behind broken doors. That August the huntsman's house stood empty as James, the kennelhuntsman, had been given notice to quit.

Horses were the staple hound food, and Tidworth roads, fields and stables were crowded with army remounts, so carcases by age or accident were plentiful. Remains from blood, fat and bones could never be cleansed from the earth-packed floor of the flesh-house. Years of grease gave it a tile-like gloss. There was only one thing to do, that was to concrete the entire site. The Sanitary Officer looked relieved, especially as Kingscote, a wealthy young man, offered to pay for the alterations. However, the Master was not satisfied, and prodded the roof with his long thumbstick. The timbers were rotten, and slates threatened to fall. Unfortunately kennels were on a repairing lease from the War Office, so Royal Engineers could not be asked to carry out the work. Kingscote was particularly worried as he was bringing his own hounds from home into kennels to start cub-hunting. More money had to be found by the Hunt.

Everyone ignored the kennels roof, being too busy reading their newspapers. In October 1918 the German navy at Wilhelmshaven mutinied on receiving orders to sail out and challenge the British navy. Allied troops were moving forward at Argonne, Champagne and Le Fère. On 11 November 1918, the Great War was over.[10]

1919 - 1925

It is unlikely that the Jazz Age reached market-town Marlborough. With butlers, footmen, grooms and gamekeepers gone to war, never to return except as remembered names on village memorials, the country house world was in deep trouble. Although arms suppliers may have made their fortunes, as they do in every conflict, many of the county families were ruined, and their houses empty. Farming was depressed, as it always is. Soldiers were out of work and roaming the roads, or selling matches in town-squares. Marlborough College continued beating boys in best *Tom Brown's Schooldays* tradition, while Captain Kingscote hunted on sixty-two days that season killing thirty-two and a half brace, with twenty-five brace run to ground.

We appear to know very little about Mr. F. C. Giddins of Crowood, Ramsbury, Master 1919-20 except that he was very popular with farmers, and ended the season with only sixteen couple hounds, with three whelps. Hounds had to be bought, an expensive pastime, and we read that Lord Ailesbury, recently returned from active service, contributed £200, with £100 from Mr. Yorke Scarlett towards the £600 required.

April 1920 meant there was no Master yet again. Only the military seemed to be in a position to help. Yorke Scarlett, chairman of a Tedworth sub-Committee, met General Sir R. G. Whigham and Brigadier General L. C. L. Oldfield, C.B., C.M.G., D.S.O., Commanding Officer at Bulford, who was renowned for helping hunting, shooting and fishing on Salisbury Plain. It was agreed that the officers should hunt the country three days a week and pay for a professional huntsman, the care of hounds and repairs to kennels. Other expenses, finds, litters, poultry-claims and earth stoppings were to be borne by the Hunt, who agreed a 2s 6d (12½p) cap. Until then, Mr. G. W. Young, with his outrageous sense of humour, had managed the kennels and earth-stopping during W.W.1., and paid poultry claims until 1924. Hounds were an anxiety, and the new Master, Sir Alfred Hickman, asked for another fifteen couples to make a viable pack.

Sir Alfred was an excellent choice, with Fred Summers as huntsman, officers and especially ladies looked forward with relish to following the 4th/7th Dragoon Guards Captain. He was on the Reserve of Officers being wounded in 1914, and was latterly Major in the Shropshire Yeomanry. Some forward Misses rode astride, to the chagrin of side-saddle skirts, aghast at such tomboyish behaviour; but peace had brought an air of freedom, with short skirts, the Blues and Charleston to an excited generation.

For army officers peacetime meant few military duties. As we were still "feeding India", garrisons at Tidworth and Bulford were reduced to cadres, and both stations were renowned for hunting, fishing on the Avon, Test or Itchen, shooting and racing. There were more invitations to parties and dances than days in the week. With a million men killed, post-war mothers were desperate, because although some daughters became brides, many were left "on the shelf" or joined the "fishing fleet" for India, as their last chance.

To deviate from chronological order, the years 1923-26 gave us the first Tedworth point-to-point at Penton. Races and names are given in detail by William Scarth Dixon in his *The Tedworth Hunt and the Tedworth Woodland Hunt* although few are memorable for this story. However, the 14th Lancers Race and the 15th/19th Hussars feature strongly. As early as 1913 the Masters of Hounds point-to-point Committee, in co-operation with the National Hunt Committee, was set up to regularise the sport, point-to-points were evolving only gradually from challenges between hunting sportsmen, in private, over natural country, with little catering for the general public. Only slowly were meetings becoming organised during the 'twenties.[11]

Of far greater interest to us when Hickman became Master, was the racecourse for amateurs constructed on Windmill Hill, Tidworth. The course lay on the south-west side facing Sidbury Hill, and adjacent to the (now disused) Tidworth-Ludgershall railway line, where it curves from a northerly direction towards the north-east. The gentle slope of the racecourse was grassland owned by the army, with a few cut-and-laid jumps together with constructed fences.[12]

Let us re-create from contemporary sources the type of meeting held at Tidworth. In April, a line of motorcars filled with officers in mufti and pretty ladies holding their hats, might have been seen winding their way up Pickpit Hill, leaving the wood and corrugated huts on the "blasted heath" of Perham Down, righthanded. No permanent brick buildings at Perham had been constructed as yet.[13] On the racecourse behind a line of official tents, gypsies traded clothes pegs, dogs barked and horses were led to the collecting ring.

Faint music from a disabled ex-serviceman's band descended on the down-draught of hill air. The comrades had walked from Andover to sell Bryant & May's matches to the sporting crowd. A small girl, dressed in a hand-knitted silk frock, stood in front of the band, pressing two pennies to her mouth, and watching the man in tattered uniform, with a peg-leg, playing a trombone. His companion, without legs, and wearing a type of leather saddle, sat on the grass beating drum and side-traps. Slowly the child walked forward, her mother watching with compassionate eyes. Standing on tiptoe she placed pennies in an empty tin, tied around a

soldier's neck. His cardboard notice pinned above war medals said:
"Blinded on the Somme".
Thin lips whispered "Thank you".

In an unsettled sky, a red biplane passed and re-passed, waggling its wings in greeting.[14] The airplane landed nearby, its cavalry officer pilot back for the weekend, jumped from the cockpit, discarded his leather flying suit to metamorphose as a happy chappie in check plus fours.

At the start, a row of General Service Waggons bordered the finishing post for the use of Hunt Committee and race officials. An Hussar fatigue assisted Mr. Fowle mount one of the waggons packed with straw bales. Living up to its name the April breeze was fresh, and the Committee with East and West side Members equally dispersed amongst the seats, looked forward to the five races with pleasant anticipation.

To Mr. Fowle this must have been very much a family affair. But then continuity has always been the essence of the Tedworth Hunt. A family affair! Mr. Assheton Smith had inherited a splendid little pack of hounds from his father Thomas G. Smith, whose ancestors had hunted Sidbury and Windmill Hills since Stuart times. On the Squire's death a Committee was formed, when again long serving families preserved the Hunt's fortunes.

Looking down the line Mr. Fowle was grateful that his kinsman Colonel E. Fowle, of Charlton Manor, with Captain C. Fowle and Andrew Fowle who had joined them, perhaps to replace the dead heir to Chute Forest.

The Marquess, over whose land hounds had hunted for a hundred years, might not have been there that day, however, F. R. Sutton Esq., of Penton Lodge, Andover, represented Sir Richard Sutton, who years past had followed Assheton Smith as Master of the Old Burton in 1824, and was his great friend and supporter.

Sir Cosmo Antrobus sat next to his near neighbour Mr. Edmunds of Cholderton. For four generations the Antrobus family were Chairmen and field Masters during eighty years. Mr. Yorke Scarlett was putting on weight! As was Captain Alexander at twenty-two stone! Even so they climbed on the waggons easily enough, to sit with Admiral Marx.

Mr. Fowle felt he could not thank the military enough. The Royal Artillery, represented on the Committee by General Oldfield and Major Cherry, Master of the R.A. (Bulford) Harriers, supported hunting during cruel war years. The cavalry at Tidworth had hunted hounds for the previous several seasons, and without help from swill-bins, horse carcasses, Colonel Hunter of the 4th Dragoon Guards, Colonel Cavendish's 9th Lancer fatigues and Major Woodhouse's 14th Hussars, foxhounds must have been put down.

With thankful eyes he remembered Hugh de Whatten, Arthur Hussey, G. Young, Mr. Ferris and Mrs. Hill, who was a very old subscriber. She always kept a fox for us and supported the Hunt very well. Little did he realise that Monty Read, a Member since 1919, together with the Read family, would be stalwarts during the next seventy years.

After the meeting was over when cars, dogcarts and farmhands on ponies braked carefully down Pickpit, a motley collection of dogs, barking gleefully, chased the vehicles. It is not known how rabies came to Wiltshire.

Perhaps an endearing mongrel had been smuggled in by a soldier home from Germany. Or a sailor maybe? During the hottest summer on record, with blazing August heat and on to November frost, all dogs and hounds had to be muzzled, so cub-hunting was lost.

By 27 November the local press reported restrictions were lifted and that:

"On Saturday the opening meet of the season will be marked by a meet at Mooltan Barracks at 11 o'clock, and as the frost has disappeared and left the ground fit, there will probably be a large company turn out."

Joyous hunting with the 4th Dragoon Guards showing the way, and 9th Lancer troopers riding second horse, came to a sudden fall. The partition of Ireland meant civil war between the Irish Free State and the Six Counties, with large troop movements from Tidworth, and the resignation of the Military Hunt Committee.

A season that started with insufficient hounds, rabies, blazing sun, frost, together with inexperienced earth-stopping, ended with no military support. April 1921 brought showers, still insufficient hounds so that more had to be purchased, the perennial question of the kennels roof, and an aptly named Miss Fairhurst, as the very first lady Master.

No wonder Yorke Scarlett, described by the Marquess as "the godfather of the Hunt", recommended Miss Fairhurst. He knew the fair lady extraordinarily well because she was joint Master with him of the Craven 1908-1919, taking over as Master 1919-21. Since John Warde and Mr. Horlock's time Craven and Tedworth have seemed to be kinsmen hunts.

Now whether Miss Fairhurst, the daughter of J. Fairhurst Esq., of Arlington Manor, Newbury, left the Craven at her previous joint Master's suggestion, or in order to be near Major General Frank K. Simmons C.B.E., M.V.O., M.C.,[15] is not known, however, it was as Mrs. Simmons at Fyfield Grange that she gave her report to the 5th March 1923 Hunt Committee at the Prince of Wales Hotel, Ludgershall.

". . . . . I do not think we need any more hounds this year," she said. The Marquess as Chairman murmured approval.

"We have thirty-seven couples in kennels* and twelve and a half couple of puppies still living, with nearly all of them having had distemper already. So they are clear."

"Must thank veterinary for that," grunted a farmer.

"But kennels and stables are in a sorry plight," she went on. "The roof is falling in." There were sighs all round.

"And what are the Royal Engineers doing about this. Eh?" questioned a member heartily sick of the subject.

"Not as easy as you think. We are on a repairing lease. And nothing to do with R.E. No! It's serious! Two days ago a shower of slates just missed hounds. Then another lot fell and nearly frightened my horse to death. It's a big job."

Mr. Sutton asked if the cost might come out of point-to-point profits, while Major Oldfield, the Treasurer, grumbled "A hundred pounds was

**Seventeen couples of draft hounds were registered in 1921, five and a half being from the Old Berkshire. Yorke Scarlett bought one and a half at a sale of Sir Watkin Wynn's hounds by Messrs. Tattersall at a sale at Rugby on 5 May 1922 for thirty-two guineas, as part of nine couple purchased.*[16]

spent last year!"

"And what does the lady Master think repairs would cost? I am rather frightened . . . . ."

"Not as frightened as I am, Mr. Whatton. You don't stand to lose any horseflesh!" There was *general laughter*.

"Thought I'd ask! It could cost two or three hundred pounds."

Lord Ailesbury waited until the merriment died down before saying:

"At the estate office we have a Clerk of the Works. An excellent fellow. Let him meet the Master and draw up a specification of things needing to be done."

"How kind!"

"Then we shall need a sub-committee to organise estimates . . . . ."

Without exception the meeting looked at Mr. Yorke Scarlett, hoping he would volunteer to sort out the matter.

Satisfactory repairs initiated through the friendship between Ailesbury and Yorke Scarlett were completed that summer, although the whole question as to whether kennels and stables be completely rebuilt on army land, or moved to a more permanent home had to be resolved!

Now how Mrs. Simmons's accident happened and what her injuries were we do not know. Everyone suspected it had something to do with "gaps", which had led to some serious mishaps. On two occasions the local paper had reported her concern over wire saying:

"She could not possibly see to it herself. The country was too big. She thought that Members of the Hunt should try and persuade farmers to make "gaps" round their farms. If young fellows would approach the farmers, as they know them better than she did, they would do it, because the Hunt was held up terribly during the season."

Let us hope that Mrs. Simmons was not badly hurt, although it put her out of hunting for six weeks, and appears to have spoilt her nerve, as she gave up the mastership after three happy seasons. Meanwhile she retained her seat on the Committee while they searched for a new Master.

Major Henry Connop, Tedworth Master 1907-08, remembered for shooting bear in the Rocky Mountains, antelope in South Africa and wearing bush kit and shiny boots, was joined in a joint Mastership by Sir Robert Leonard Powell of Flowers Hill, Pangbourne, for 1924-5 season only. Powell was a fine whip and member of the Coaching Club.[17] A newspaper report says that his beautiful team of bays kept at the Ailesbury Arms, Marlborough, were much admired. A picture of a meet at West Close, his house, together with hounds and a small field, appears in William Scarth Dixon's book. One wonders if either Connop or Powell owned a printing works! In a beautiful printed letter they proposed hunting the combined East and West sides three times a week, and this clearly being in the Hunt's best interest, there was pleasant approval all round.

No hunt reports from these years survive, which is disappointing. Huntsmen are inclined to lock away their diaries, so that in old age they can once again savour triumphs, failure and disappointments, while they sit by the fireside in wheelchairs, dog on knee. Their families do not understand the value of these important documents which describe, as no other record can, the social history of our English country scene.

One sensation lingers on the magnetic breath of Tidworth. Hounds were perturbed that day. They jumped up and whined, paws on walls. Horses were restive as animals know the ending of an era instinctively, when never again will anything be quite the same.

Breakfast over in the mess, every military band in the garrison was playing, the sound circling from Ashdown Copse to Sidbury. Claredon to Dunch. Tedworth House woke and glittered to say farewell.

The 17th/21st Lancers had packed up and were leaving for Aldershot. The entire regiment, in mounted sections, was led by the commanding officer mounted on a grey horse:

"With lance-flags fluttering, lance points glinting in the sun and all officers with swords drawn, it must have been a fine sight. Crowds gathered as the bands of the 12th Lancers and 14th/20th Hussars led the parade through the village. On reaching Perham Down the accompanying bands and troops pulled away with a final cheer."[18]

The next year brought the General Strike and the start of social revolution.

PART II

Chapter 7

The Tedworth Woodland Foxhounds

During the 1923-24 season it was agreed that the Godfather should hunt the great woods of Wiltshire and Hampshire in our country. The story of the Tedworth Woodland Hunt belongs to the second part of this book, as it is set in the 'twenties and 'thirties. This period exemplifies the shifting social pattern of British country sport.

Yorke Scarlett loved forest venery. Perhaps also there was a desire on his part to concentrate on one particular part of country, and to breed a pack specifically devoted to this purpose. It is only a master hunting hounds himself, who knows what 'sort' suits him best. The confusion caused by endless changes of mastership from civilian to military and back again, made hounds as nonplussed as their unfortunate huntsmen.

The Grand Avenue, Savernake

The meet of Tedworth Woodland foxhounds at Durley House.
L to R: Mr. Yorke Scarlett, M.F.H., Lady Yarrow, M.F.H., and Ted Hope, kennel huntsman.

In the 1924 summer garden of Fyfield House,* woven cane chairs of pre-WWI vintage might have been grouped around an equally venerable Edwardian table. The Scarletts led a conventional country life rooted in the traditions of the English squirearchy. Whisky and iced-lemonade would have been placed on it by the Scarlett's Scots parlour-maid, lately travelled from Gigha to 'see the world'.

After the war, Scarlett money was not too plentiful, so they were forced to sell the island to Major John Allen, a frequent visitor to Gigha in halcyon "Snapshot" days. And, hence the welcome given by the kind Scarlett family to many little maids who looked upon service at Fyfield as an open door to the wide world.

Lady Yarrow was expected. She lived at Green Meadows, Goodworth Clatford, and was a keen hunting lady. When she arrived at the front door with its stone columns and ornate balcony, she would have been met by Yorke Scarlett because this was to be a propitious day. He might have taken both her hands, and as they passed, talking earnestly, into the garden on the front of the light-coloured house, was, we wonder, the white rose blooming in the corner? Or like its counterpart "New Dawn" flowering by the steps between the massive triple windows of the drawing-room and dining-room, a later planting?[1]

The garden is sweet-scented with sycamore, chestnut and maple sheltering the lawn from wind. Perhaps a pony grazed in the paddock past the greenhouse, because the Scarletts were not great gardeners, and staff was becoming unaffordable. Seated in cane chairs, the friends would have discussed Amy Fairhurst's wedding to Simmons, and the unfortunate fact that she only hunted hounds twice a week. The Guarantee of £600 was insufficient for her to employ a professional huntsman, and hunt the entire country. Therefore the great woodlands of West Woods, Collingbourne, Doles and Harewood were fast becoming neglected scrubland, and out of hand from a foxhunting point of view. During the 1923-24 season woodlands were alive with foxes. Only careful pruning and hunting half-forgotten paths could rescue them from sprouting hazel growing amidst thorn and bracken. These must have been subjects discussed in the Fyfield garden.

Mrs. Yorke Scarlett, the Secretary of the newly formed Tedworth Woodland Hunt, walked down Portland stone steps from the house. She must have been as keen as her husband that Lady Yarrow accept a joint Mastership, because she knew that her husband needed a charming lady with a sweet smile, to deal with tiresome Tedworth subscribers.

Kind and generous though he was, Yorke Scarlett wished to hunt hounds without chattering voices to break the stillness. More and more he craved the solitude of his delectable woodland. His great-nephew Jonathan Scarlett tells us that his uncle liked to lose the field, and hunt alone with Charlie Perrin as whipper-in. As Charlie's father came with Mr. Shrubb in 1891, long association made a strong bond between the two men. Perhaps he alone understood the loss of Gigha. No longer had he the absorbing interest of the management of the island, and the friendship of its inhabitants he

**o.s. ref. 292466*

cared for so well. Gone was "Snapshot", summer vacations, the Agricultural Show, Clydesdales winning at Campbelltown, flowers, blue sea and white sand. Thus it must have been with considerable pleasure and relief to the Scarletts that Lady Yarrow accepted their invitation to join them at the helm of the Tedworth Woodland.

Before dinner they would have gone back into Fyfield House, leased so many times to an assortment of masters, as a home during their short periods of office with the Hunt.

Jonathan Scarlett remembers the house when he visited it as a boy, with the silver rosebowl presented to his great-uncle on the side-table. We imagine that a little maid would have led Lady Yarrow through the hall lit by oil lamps, with its smell of oilcloth, paraffin and boiled mutton, and up the stairs. Fawn-painted walls were dressed with foxes' masks, and the new joint Master was not able to decide if there were fifty or sixty sharp noses, with bead eyes gazing into the past, as flames flickered upon cotton-plaited wicks to give a haunting woodland light. Perhaps she felt amused at the patient care with which the girl poured hot water into a china washbasin. There were no upstairs taps in the Scarlett household. And but one tap in the kitchen. Sea-storms; the swish of Gigha palm-trees seemed to permeate the old house.

The following morning the two Masters would most probably have visited hounds. Thirty couple were kennelled at Appleshaw, a small village about two and a half miles north-east of Fyfield. E. Hope was kennelhuntsman with W. Swann second whipper-in to Perrin.

A photograph shows Mr. Scarlett wearing his ancient tweed hat and Burberry, standing with eager hounds, gazing into his face with trust and absolute affection. In common with some far-seeing masters, notably the great hound-breeder Sir Edward Curry, he had been turning thoughts towards introducing a percentage of Welsh blood into hounds. This is partly a reaction against the dominance of the Belvoir-type where the craze for bone meant shoulders were suffering and activity lost.

Several very early photographs show Woodland hounds clearly defined against the stucco wall of kennels. The Welsh influence is unmistakeable. There are the slightly domed heads of Diamond and Artemis, while Bonnylass has a wise expression, because the hound is highly intelligent and full of character. Burbage, and many others have the tendency to rough coats. You can see the joy that Yorke Scarlett feels in breeding the type he wanted to hunt his favourite forest.

His hounds are entered first in the 1928 F.K.S.B., with draft hounds from the Radnor & W. Hereford, Newaddfawr, Tickham, Sir W. Wynn's, Gelligaer & Tallybont, Carmarthenshire, V.W.H. (Cricklade), Mr. Curre's and, importantly, the Wheatland and two Craven bitches.

By 1929 and 1930 he is using Archer '23 from the Radnor & W. Hereford extensively on Wheatland and Craven bitches, also the famous Tedworth Plaintiff '27 (Berkeley Waggoner '22 on Berkeley Purity '24). A similar pattern is shown in the early 'thirties.

Returning from Appleshaw and later that day, Lady Yarrow would have driven the seven miles to her home at Goodworth Clatford. Narrow winding

Meet of Tedworth Woodland Hunt at Fairway.
L to R: Lady Rosemary Brudenell-Bruce, Ted Hope, Lord and Lady Cardigan (standing), Mr. and Mrs. Selwyn (standing), Charlie Perrin (mounted), Mr. Yorke Scarlett, Sir Richard (later Lord) Wright, Sir W. and Lady Fuller, Mrs. Byron (in front with hound).

lanes were overhung with autumn beech hedges glowing scarlet, orange and lemon. Eleanor Yarrow was the second wife of Sir Alfred Fernandez Yarrow, Bart.,[2] F.R.S., M.I.C.E., the famous engineer and shipbuilder. She married him in 1922, a mere three months after the death of his first wife. The Yarrow motto is:

"Be Just and Fear Not. Sans Dieu Rien."[3]

So they must have been friends and impervious to local gossip. Although not a young woman, Eleanor's figure is lithe and graceful.

Today you can cross by a wooden bridge over the sparkling water of the river Anton, a tributary of the glorious Test. Trout and grayling flick amongst streaming weed on a sandy bed. Passing a clipped box hedge you enter a fairy-green world, a garden of water, moss-green grass and ornamental trees in rose-madder dresses. Green Meadows was once a corn mill, and the millstream splits from the Anton to form an island haven for fishermen. The house is built astride the stream. A 1926 photograph shows a meet with the Master and Secretary, Lieutenant Colonel Eady, O.B.E., riding bay horses with the red brick, red tiled house in the background. A thatched petrol-house stands by itself. We cannot distinguish Lady Yarrow's face.

The principal meeting places of the Woodland were at Biddesden Gate, Crawlboys Farm, Fox Inn, Tangley, Durley Gate, and for Savernake, Leigh Hill, Postern Gate and Eight Walks. Interesting photographs show a meet at Leigh Hill House.

The Master sits on his horse to the left of the picture. A large majestic figure with a moustache and wearing a monocle, he is saying little to ladies in long, fur-trimmed coats who stand in the background. The men present wear breeches or tweeds and soft hats. A nanny with a veil guards two small children, keeping them well away from the pack of Welsh cross-breds. As we have seen many hounds show the coarse coats of their breeding.

In this picture, Lady Yarrow takes centre-stage. A black-clad figure riding astride, the cut of her coat is very long to show the outline of her figure. She wears a tophat, with white or pale hair sticking out each side of the brim. Maybe she was younger than the picture suggests, or even quite pretty, but the hair and the hat give her an appearance like CoCo the clown! Although the expression is sweet. And is that a small monkey-puzzle tree we can see nestling beside the oak?

Hounds have moved off to the front of Leigh Hill House built for Ailesbury estate workers, although Henry the fifth Marquess lived here in 1909.[4] Another photograph shows the house completely swathed in creeper. It faces front, ahead of a zig-zag of five or six brick and thatched cottages. Today damp brick walls are tile-hung, and with its slate roof it is large, clammy and cold. Mr. Scarlett, his hounds Traffic, Graceful, Caroline and Chairman gathered round him, sits his hunter, his heavy, slightly slouched figure, with legs cocked forward in an old-fashioned way, he typifies one of the last of a dying breed of men.

He moves off across moss-choked lawns, brilliant in the sunshine. The demesne is ringed with encroaching beech, ash trees and oak. Ivy-carpets soften the feet of wood-post fences, coated green by lichen the colour of baby lettuce. Today our monkey-puzzle stands tall and imposing. An attractive photograph shows Lady Rosemary Brudenell-Bruce riding Nimble, standing next to Mr. Blanchard.

Still another photo of the same day depicts the Master taking his pack by a long line of elm trees sheltering an open meadow. Charlie Perrin, riding in front, has a wicked grin on his face. What mischief has been brewed up by this close-thinking pair? How long, one wonders, will their field hold-up tree-arched paths, alert, we hope, with good holloas.

We do not know the hunt plan for the day except that a photograph shows them coming down Column Vista. The Master would have drawn slowly and carefully, and he had the uncanny ability to anticipate the run of a fox. Pheasants scuttled by, while a weasel crossed swiftly fearing young entry might be hungry! The Amity Oak, with its owl and woodpecker is taller today than it was in Yorke Scarlett's time.

This is a magic fern-brushed place, and we are sure hounds stooped to their task on weak woodland scent, their free and musical voices causing overtones in vertical air-columns of the forest.

As Ikey Bell describes:

"These Welsh cross breds will quest and work up to a fox in a woodland on the faintest of overnight drags, and are therefore good finders, being wide-ranging and inquisitive by nature."

Hunting experts believe that foxes in forests such as Savernake would do with a great deal more rattling than they get. No subscription was ever taken to hunt with the Tedworth Woodland, the Scarletts bearing the entire expense. The only proviso being that the field must belong to the Tedworth Hunt.

Quoting from *A Huntsman's Logbook* makes one remember that in 1925 Isaac Bell came to hunt the South and West Wilts. A very strange man, he was exceptionally tall and thin, and was an American educated at Harrow. He had a hard-riding wife, who practically invented event racing, and took a glorious black eye to Buckingham Palace, after her horse failed a five-bar gate. He also had a daughter Diana.[5] She proved her iron-nerve at sixteen years old by winning the Berks and Bucks Open Ladies' Race, and lots more races on horses trained by her intrepid cheese-grater mother.[6]

Ikey is pertinent to our story because he and Yorke Scarlett intensely disliked each other. His great-nephew confirms this, as do others who knew them. Perhaps Ikey disliked ex-West Indies sugar barons? Or Scarlett hated the prevalent American boast of:

"We won the war!"

Perhaps the truth was that Scarlett was a father figure, who became a great friend of the Duke of Beaufort. Photographs collected by Miss Joan Wasey show Lord Ailesbury, Lady Cardigan and Mr. Yorke Scarlett with the Duke and his famous hounds. Scarlett was tolerant of youthful lunatics such as Farquhar, Lady Dulverton, then Ruth Farquhar, and Dickie Fanshawe. In contrast Bell was a hard man. If you liked him and his family all was well. Otherwise they were inclined to put up your hackles. Acid and intolerant, both he and Scarlett were experimenting with Welsh-cross blood.

The meet of the Duke of Beaufort's hounds at Tottenham House circa 1930.
L to R (mounted): Lord Ailesbury, Mr. Yorke Scarlett, the Duke of Beaufort.

The meet of the Duke of Beaufort's hounds at Tottenham House.
L to R: Lady Cardigan is holding a whip with Captain Powell wearing a top hat. Mr. Yorke Scarlett is talking to Mr. Porter, while Mr. Kemble stands by the column smiling.

However, Lady Dulverton, who knows more about hounds than anyone, believes that whereas the Tedworth Woodland pack was slower with beautiful music, Bell's hounds were quick and fast.

Spiteful Ikey certainly was. Captain H. V. Sanderson R.A., army chaplain, and deputy Master to Major Scott-Watson, R.A. (Bulford) Harriers, describes in his letter a chance meeting between the American and Scarlett. Both hunting their fox, the two packs became mixed up! According to Bell, Yorke Scarlett's attempts on his horn, as he describes afterwards, were like noises made by a "syphilitic cow"! And his attempts to separate his hounds absolutely pathetic! Ikey was laughing too hard to do anything to help. This sounds far-fetched, considering Scarlett's long and honoured experience.

They say that this peculiar huntsman Ikey Bell became carried away, and inebriated at hunt dinners. It appears he broke his hip after falling from a high rooftruss, and crashing down onto the top table. Let us hope the beef and gravy had been cleared away. After that he rode side-saddle during one cub-hunting season. And when confined to a wheelchair he clutched a tiny Pekingese dog to an aching heart.[7]

The 3 February 1932 gave the Woodland a good hunt from the coverts of Savernake Outliers, a group of woods to the east of the Forest. That day Lady Yarrow had the whole-hearted sympathy of all followers on the recent death of her husband Sir Alfred.

Scent was good and a fox from the Pleasure Grounds at Tottenham House was lucky to make good his escape![8] A substitute from Bedwyn Common did not share such good fortune. He had evidently been on the

Meet of Tedworth Woodland hounds at Durley House.
L to R: Miss Joan Wasey, Mrs. Vigors, Mr. Peter Scarlett.

move as hounds in their wide-ranging way, being good finders, did not work up to him for some time. After some persevering work in coverts they got on better terms, and with a great cry drove hard to Stokke Common, then swung sharp round to Bedwyn Common again, and over London Ride to Warren Road. At this point the fox was headed by Chisbury Cottages, where he ran left-handed over the open to Knowle Hill and Belmore with hounds close behind him. Facing the open once more he skirted the edge of Birch Copse, and while pointing for Bedwyn Common hounds caught a view and rolled him over before he could reach covert. The time was fifty minutes, and hounds set a great pace for a most enjoyable gallop.

The story of this generous little Woodland pack was coming to its close. Eleanor, Lady Yarrow in her widowhood, was depressed and becoming restless. The two Masters for 1933-34 were joined by Captain R. P. L. Vigors D.S.O., and Mrs. Vigors of East Kennet Manor. From a picture of a meet at Durley House, the home of Sir Robert and Lady Wright, one sees an athletic, hard-riding woman with an aquiline nose and weather-beaten face. The revers of her side-saddle coat are cut long and low to display a silk hunting-tie to elegant advantage.

"She was a lovely lady, vivacious and very kind to us children," says Mr. Jim Read. "Captain Vigors was more austere. He wore a bunch of Parma violets in his buttonhole, and always smoked a Havana cigar. The smoke wafted back to us children, and we thought it lovely."

He goes on:

"When the War came there were money problems. So they left East Kennet, and took 'a sort of farm' near Minehead. After her husband died Mrs. Vigors became Master of the Minehead Harriers 1956-59."[9]

With great regret the resignation of Eleanor, Lady Yarrow was accepted by the Committee in 1936. She was to leave the country. Her husband being a well-known shipbuilder perhaps she went on a cruise, to live in a warmer climate. It was sad to see her go. Lady Wright, M.F.H. Tedworth 1935-37, took over with Mr. Yorke Scarlett for two seasons, until the Tedworth Woodland was disbanded in 1938-39 season.

Photograph of painting of Tedworth Woodland hounds by Miss B. Shiffner.
"Bridegroom and his sons, 1929."
L to R: Bloxham, Burbage, Bedwyn, Bridegroom (centre light hound), Bellman, Bedlam, Baffler, Burgundy, Batchelor, Boreham (in front).

Chapter 8

Sir Peter Farquhar and Lord Melchett 1923 – 1934

Peter Farquhar's terriers meant almost more to him than his beloved foxhounds.

Returning to 1923, at Tedworth kennels the bands had stopped playing, because 17th/21st Lancers have forsaken Tidworth for Aldershot. There is a feeling of anti-climax. Hounds are despondent, and there are few of them, as distemper slaughters puppies wholesale. Controversy seemed to be in the air, with the clash of personalities that bedevils any Hunt.

Colonel Fowle was unhappy.

"It would be a retrograde step," he said, "to get a gentleman such as Mr. Kemble to hunt hounds in this wire-entangled country."

"This is the third committee meeting we've had since Sir Leonard Powell resigned," sighed the Chairman. "And still we can't agree."

"Connop knows the country and has had long experience. And even if on many occasions he did not get his fox, it was better for Charlie!" There was laughter all round. "Connop can hunt as sole Master. I cannot see the difficulty."

"But Major Connop will not hunt the West Side," interposed Hugh Whatton. "That's why I voted for Kemble last time, even though Connop is a good friend to the Hunt. Kemble's agreed to hunt the country as a whole."

Mr. Fowle put in: "Kemble comes from a very old Essex family."

"Irrelevant!" snorted his cousin. "He's never hunted hounds!"

"He's perfectly competent to take hounds, though he's never actually hunted them before. And he's proposing to hunt both sides now."

In the end Colonel Fowle was over-ruled and Mr. A. K. E. Kemble was appointed for the 1923-24 season, and also the following year. A guarantee of £1,000 was offered, generously topped up to £1,200 by Sir Leonard Powell.

Not only had Kemble never hunted a pack but he was no houndman, with disastrous results. After his short time the Tedworth kennels were almost empty. There was nothing left! Which shows it only takes two years to destroy a tradition.

On a kinder note, a photograph of a meet at The Crown, Everleigh, shows a pleasant enough personage, riding a pale grey horse named Lady Jane, and this photo gives a good opportunity to look at Everleigh country. It stands at a turning-ridge or backbone. Spreading northwards like a fan lies Pewsey Vale, Savernake and away on to Collingbourne Forest. Then Chute Causeway leads to Andover. To the south of Everleigh lies Salisbury Plain proper.

On the day that horses and hounds were photographed in front of the square white Georgian hotel, sounds of firing were heard, because the Plain was active every weekday. Wind ruffled spruce and chalk-bleached herbs. A sharp, active thoroughbred horse, near the ground, with some pony blood, was considered best for the empty grassland of Everleigh. The village is clothed with trees for warmth, and today Forestry Commission plantations give form and outline to loneliness. Perhaps it was a credit to the Master's tenacity that he completed his short time of office in spite of foot-and-mouth disease, frost and snow.

That spring, fate in the form of young Peter Farquhar came to Mooltan Barracks, Tidworth. Returning from India and the Scots Greys where he had become very ill and nearly died, Peter went to Ireland on convalescent leave. Although he could ride, he had not hunted very much, and thought Irish hunting tremendous fun. Posted to 16th/5th Lancers, he soon discovered this little pack of Tedworth foxhounds in kennels, and asked his Colonel, the very charming Geoffry Brooke:

"Sir, if I do Orderly Officer every weekend may I hunt hounds?"[1] Colonel Brooke, who may have guessed that this young man was destined to go far, agreed and today most hunting people have heard of Sir Peter Farquhar, sixth Baronet. He inherited the title from his father, who was killed in action in 1918.

Permission granted, the following letter was sent to the Honorary Secretary, Admiral Marx:

"Dear Sir,

I am writing to offer to take the Tidworth hounds next season, on the following conditions:

(1) That I shall hunt the country five days a fortnight, and a bye.

(2) That I shall hunt the hounds myself with an amateur first whip, Mr. Fanshawe, 16th/5th Lancers, and a professional second whip.

(3) If I hunt the hounds five days a fortnight and a bye, the Committee shall give me £1,000 a year.

(4) That the Committee be responsible for the upkeep and rates of the kennels and for poultry claims, etc., also for the upkeep of the country and coverts and wire fund and for litters and finds, etc.

Yours sincerely

Peter Farquhar."

The letter was greeted with enthusiasm, and even Colonel Fowle was pleased. Young, keen and intensely ambitious, Peter visited every farmer in the district, as this was the best way to have foxes preserved. Hounds, however, were few in number and poor quality. There were only eight couple in kennels, and of these three and a half had to be put down due to old age or unsoundness. On a sour note, Mr. Kemble was asked to contribute £100 in some compensation for the twenty-four and a half couple he had agreed to hand over to the Committee.

Drafts had to be acquired immediately, both good old hounds who knew their work and unentered puppies. So Peter went shopping. A new-found friend in Ikey Bell gave him drafts from the South and West Wilts. He also acquired drafts from Sir Ian Heathcoat Amory of the Tiverton as well as the Heythrop and Brocklesby.[2]

Daphne Moore in *The Book of the Foxhound* tell us us that he visited Berkeley Castle to inspect hounds he had purchased from them.

"On leaving he happened to see a half-grown puppy, very ill with pneumonia, and was told by the huntsman that it was the best-bred in the kennel, combining the famous lines of Berkeley Waggoner 1922, a grandson of Whipcord 1912 . . . and Berkeley Plunder 1918, sire of Playmate 1924 and his sister Purity, who was the dam of the sick puppy. Sir Peter, on hearing his breeding, was determined to save his life and have him for his own, so, since the chances of the puppy's survival were negligible in kennel, he was 'thrown-in' with the draft and recovered. In the words of Sir Peter, 'his great courage and constitution pulled him through'. Plaintiff entered at the Tedworth . . . became an outstanding foxhound."

Peter's sister Ruth, Lady Dulverton, who lived near Newbury and came down to hunt, says that Dick Fanshawe, whom she later married, together with Peter's youngest brother, whipped-in. Captain Richard Fanshawe became Master of the South Oxfordshire 1938-47. R. E. Field-Marsham and R. M. Fanshawe also whipped-in as military commitments allowed.

They were carefree, happy days, with a young Master. He wanted his field to enjoy themselves and to take part. Peter tried to make people aware of hunting for its own sake, and not just to come out for the riding. Activating people to play their part, whether they are "doggy" or not, is a flair. He felt that everybody should have a ringside seat, to watch hounds draw, and hunt their fox in all types of country.[3]

One of the great compliments Peter paid to Dick, in later years, was that he had had a great many whippers-in. "But not one who could hold a candle to Dickie." He thought day and night about hunting. He studied it down the ages, and had a very retentive memory.

Things do not always follow to plan, and that first season field manners left much to be desired! Farmers complained of galloping over spring barley, and gates being left open for cattle to stray. Peter told the Committee about his difficulties in controlling an unruly field, particularly on Salisbury Plain. And it was agreed that Sir Leonard Powell be invited to resume the post of field Master.

Lady Dulverton says that her brother, who is now regarded as a pioneer breeder of the modern foxhound, was a disciple of Ikey Bell. As Master of the South and West Wilts Foxhounds, he bred a pack that was to change the size, shape and weight of the modern foxhound. Using a proportion of Welsh blood, in 1928, the famous S. and W.W. Godfrey by Kilkenny Gory out of Carlow Goosecap was given to Bell as a present. Later this celebrated stallion hound was used by both Farquhar and the Duke of Beaufort.[4] Bell is remembered as the breeder who made Welsh blood fashionable in England, he set the trend because traditionalists always regarded Sir Edward Curre, the progressive and immortal hound-breeder, as a mere Welshman![5]

It is fascinating to consider the Scarlett/Farquhar/Bell relationship. First the august Godfather with his majestic hounds on their long, woodland hunts.

Peter Farquhar hunting Tedworth hounds in Savernake Forest, 6 December 1929.

"It was a lovely sound hunting in Savernake," says Lady Dulverton. Yorke Scarlett was very tolerant of young lunatics like us! And a marvellous friend to foxhunting."

Then there was Ikey Bell, the respected, unusual Master in his middle forties. He was content to have a young convert worshipping at his feet; but there was sharp grit in his attitude towards the venerable Scarlett.

At the same time, Peter in his first season to carry the horn, had the excitement, freshness and desire to produce hounds that, like Bell's, were quick and alert, and was laying the foundation of breeding a good pack at Tidworth.

Hunting in Savernake, Plaintiff, restored from pneumonia to outstanding strength and fitness, leapt the high deer-fence to make good the ground when the pack had checked. And then jumped it back again. He was the only hound in the pack who could clear this fence, and did it on several occasions in the course of a hunt[6]

Plaintiff again excelled himself the following season.

"At the finish of a memorable Boxing Day hunt of eighteen miles, Plaintiff led the pack at the end of one hour twenty-five minutes' hunting and, driving on at a great pace, overhauled their beaten fox."[7]

The next year Peter was joined by the honorable Henry Mond, who was to become the second Lord Melchett in 1931. His photograph shows an alert young man, wearing a velvet hunting cap, dark in features and colouring. He has a sensitive face with full lips. A well-known business man, Henry lived at Woodfalls, Romsey, and found time to help the Tedworth during the next five years.

The Baer Meyer Mond family was of Lithuanian Jewish extraction originating from Cassel. His grandfather, Ludwig Mond, was a chemist and industrialist who came to England in 1862 to found the Mond Nickel Company. His father, Alfred Moritz Mond, founded Brumer Mond & Co. to synthesize ammonia used in the manufacture of ammonium nitrate for explosives. He was Chairman of I.C.I., Director of Nobel Industries, also the Westminster Bank. His motto was:

"Make Yourself Necessary."[8]

He became Minister of Health in 1921-22,[9] and reconstructed Melchett Court, a palatial Jacobean mansion near Romsey, for himself and his wife Violet. Henry's mother spoke English with difficulty, and always with a guttural[10] accent. Woodfalls was built especially for him, and Henry took over many of his father's directorships.

Henry suffered with a bad heart. Visiting South Africa, he came ill, and returned home in 1920 with his nurse Gwen née Wilson, who had married him. A keen fisherman, the peace of the River Test was an antidote to a stormy marriage; together with acerbic repercussions from the Wall Street financial crisis[11] Then Henry was introduced to Peter and he 'found' hunting![12]

"Henry Mond was a splendid man," says Lady Dulverton. "Hunting was new to him and he was more enthusiastic and interested than you can possibly imagine. His enthusiasm was started when he met Peter, so that later when he became Master of the Oakley he bred a very good pack of hounds himself.

Hunt Ball 1930 at Tedworth House.
L to R: Alastair Gibb, Peter Sykes, Henry Melchett, Peter Farquhar, ... Roselli, Mike Farquhar, Reg Farquhar.
Ladies: Lilah Daly, Ruth Farquhar, Victoria Fuller, Lady Ernest St. Maur, Verity Holroyd, Mrs. Roselli.

"Henry so enjoyed himself out hunting! He was a heavyweight and rode lovely big horses. He did not ride tremendously well, and depended on Peter to get him good horses, and let them carry him along. He was a busy man and hunting was a brief relaxation between periods of industrial life. He was an exuberant, unlikely sort of character.

"Also he had very bad eyesight, and said he was going to invent little windscreen-wipers to clean his glasses." Lady Dulverton goes on: "We used to pull his leg and ask him how the invention was getting along!"

"Henry was naive in a way, and his enjoyment in hunting was unbelieveable. A very generous man, he was completely carried away by the whole thing."

This was the first long mastership since 1909 and gave a period of stability. Together they bred one of the best packs of hounds the Hunt has ever had. Plaintiff, as well as being excellent in his work, proved an outstanding sire. His best daughter was Tedworth Pastry '30 out of Faculty '28, drafted from the Heythrop. Faculty's dam Heythrop Fairmaid '23, her tail-female traces to Sir Thomas Mostyn's Lady '01.

Later Pastry was mated with Soûth and West Wilts' Phoenix '28. His was the connecting link between Welsh blood and the orthodox breeding of 1930 packs. From this mating the celebrated Meynell Pageant '35 was bred by Peter after he left the Tedworth, taking Plaintiff and Pastry with him. Pageant is regarded as the cornerstone on which many modern kennels are built.[13]

In 1929 the 16th/5th Lancers left Tidworth, so Peter resigned his commission and rented Middlecot House, Quarley, for two years. This is on the east side of the country, and hunted only as frequently as the fox population would allow.

The house looked out across fields to the Roman Fort, where pheasants strut. Stables still exist, although the house is no more. Peter found that although Lewis Edmunds, Esq., of Cholderton, was a great friend to foxhunting and always saved Charlie for us, other shooting syndicates were not kind to foxes.

Peter was a frequent visitor to Woodfalls, travelling from Grateley station to Romsey, where Henry's chauffeur remembers meeting the train. The household was run with great extravagance. The dining room had a false floor, which slid back to reveal a swimming pool, constructed in the cellar, which was a tremendous innovation at that date. Time often appeared meaningless, as dinner ordered for eight o'clock was often not eaten till midnight.[14] Hunting was the great solace to Henry's woes.

A letter written from Woodfalls by Peter on 11 February 1931 to Mr. Fowle describes how difficult things had been for Lord Melchett after his father's death! Also that he, Peter, had received a very attractive offer to go to the Meynell, so that he was unable to put in an offer for the following season.

"I am very sorry indeed about it as I have thoroughly enjoyed myself here and everyone has been more than kind to me and I hate the thought of leaving.

Yours sincerely
Peter Farquhar."

To everyone's regret, Peter left the Tedworth and his home at Quarley. Nothing remains of Middlecot House itself. Like its famous counterpart "The Ruins", this ancient fourteen-room house built in brick and chalk, was burnt soon after Peter left to become Master of the Meynell. With no water to quench the flames the Andover fire brigade stood by helplessly as tinder-dry roof trusses collapsed and blazing thatch poured into upstairs rooms. Today you can still see the outline of the house, secret beneath scrambling ivy, with an oven and fireplace where the Master dried wet boots after the rigours of Windy Dido. And in the frost the best garden snowdrops flower in the whole wide world.[15]

Mr. John C. Porter, of Sunnyhill, near Milton,* was Secretary throughout Peter's Mastership, when East and West sides were combined once more. Porter succeeded Admiral Marx, who during WW1 rejoined the Navy as a lieutenant. Appointed to a minesweeper, Marx was promoted Commander to his intense joy! This was fifty years after attaining that rank fifty years before. Tragically, in 1926, the Admiral was drowned in a sailing accident.[16]

To Lord Melchett's and the Committee's evident satisfaction, he soon wrote to Mr. Porter to say that he and Major A. E. Phillips, D.S.O., of Elm House, Winterbourne Dauntsey, then joint Master of the South Berks, [17] were prepared to carry on the pack and this excellent arrangement lasted until 1934.

A quiet, unassuming man, Phillips was a great help to Henry, even though he did not make a great impression either out hunting or with the 'management'. However, he loved hunting and was a solid back-up to Henry.[18]

In a brown photograph album with a silk tie, Hark For'ard in the local newspaper proclaimed:

"Tedworth in luck. Sparkling Performance with an Afternoon Fox."

He continues: "The curtain rang up for the regular season at Rainscombe Park, by invitation of Sir Ashley and Lady Biggs."

A photograph shows patches of late sunlight through oak, beech and venerable cedar, still in leaf. Lord Melchett on a grey hunter leads a large field through handsome parkland to the coverts on spectacular Oare Hill. Hark For'ard goes on:

"Scent proved poor and nothing much was done until the afternoon when hounds put up a sparkling performance.

Getting away on good terms with a fox from some rushes near New Mill, they raced away over a nice line, pointing for Easton Royal, short of which they crossed the Burbage-Pewsey road and swung right-handed nearly to Milton. Then, turning up the flank of Easton Hill, they went on towards Everleigh, on the Plain; but the pressure was too great and the fox turned sharp back to the Vale, hounds rolling him over on the precipitous side of Milton Hill. Time twenty-five minutes without a check or touching a covert."

The huntsman that season was Dick Fanshawe, recently returned to Tidworth from Edinburgh. He loved the hounds and had a quiet authoritative control over them. Being a very quick, active man, his brain was usually a jump ahead of the fox![19] At New Mill and guessing the line Charlie would take he must have shepherded hounds across the railway line to safety. A precision rider over five-barred gates of the Vale, Dick was a superb rider, and he was uncatchable galloping the grass of Easton Hill, towards Everleigh.

Returning to stables that night he would have brought his horse home "without a peck on him!" as they say in Wiltshire.

**The postal address has changed since that date.*

Opening meet at Rainscombe Park, 31 October 1931.
L to R: Derek Mond, Major Phillips, M.F.H., Lady Melchett, Lord Melchett, M.F.H., "Tubby" Cooper (King's Dragoon Guards), Dick Fanshawe (16th Lancers), two whippers-in.

Henry's health caused great concern during these years. At the beginning of 1932 Major Phillips was in sole command for the first few weeks, as Henry had been ordered a prolonged rest, although at the Manningford meet everyone was delighted to see Lord Melchett back in the saddle and completely recovered from his long illness.

That bleak December Colonel Fowle died. Every Wiltshire foxhunter paid his or her respect at his funeral, with the enormous crowd showing deep sorrow at the passing of one of the old school, who loved and was always doing everything he could for the chase.

Captain (later Brigadier) M. W. Selby-Lowndes, D.S.O., R.A., was amateur huntsman when Dick Fanshawe moved from Tidworth. On 21 December 1933 before a meet at Netheravon, he would have come down to breakfast at Greenlands Farm, a detachment of the School of Artillery, Larkhill, responsible for maintenance and safety of the Ranges. As messing member of the mess at Greenlands, the Captain was notorious for feeding his fellow officers on Camp coffee and rabbit pie for sixpence a day! This morning, however, there were bacon and eggs because it was Christmas![20]

After breakfast, the huntsman mounted his horse and stood for a while watching his men with their waggons and heavy horses set out to tramp the weary miles to search the Ranges for unexploded shells.[21] A labour which never ceases. When grey December nor'easters blow snow-mist from Ell Barrow to Charlton Down the Plain is a hard, rough place. For that reason Tedworth hounds rarely hunted over the impact area, although our country extends as far as the old coach road from Salisbury to Foxley Corner. This meet at Netheravon was exceptional and one of the only accounts of a classic hunt over the Ranges.

After hacking to the meet by way of Blackball Firs and Wexland Hanging, Selby-Lowndes slowly drew the high ground, to put up a tough customer in some rough grass near Lavington Folly. Getting away on his brush, hounds raced to Slay Down, the bitter winds slashing the faces of both horse and rider. Left-handed slipped Charlie past Enford Pennings to Shrewton Folly, where the only check occurred. Here the look and shape of the land changes. Icy winds play tricks with streaming eyes, while thistle seeds blow about the treeless landscape, and trillions of ants bore minute tunnels in dry, parched ground.

A view of his fox running ancient trackways got things going again, and hounds ran on hard to the Urchfont road, then up again to Ell Barrow and Charlton Down. Here an open earth on the ridge above Water Dean Bottom put an end to the fastest hunt of the season. A distance of nine miles in all.

Hacking home in darkness, Selby-Lowndes and his whipper-in called to see the redoubtable giant Captain W. Howard Alexander. Now weighing twenty stone, he was as devoted to hunting as when he whipped-in to the Tedworth in First World War days. Supper was excellent, and the friends talked fox-hunting till three in the morning, before falling asleep in their chairs.[22]

Like his great friend Arthur Hussey, "Tiny" Alexander liked to hunt the hare, so he founded the Pewsey Vale Beagles, a beautiful little pack of fourteen-and-a-half-inch hounds kennelled at Upavon. When Tiny was too stout to hunt, he gave them to Henry's sons Derek and Julian. Derek, a smart, bright boy, loved to whip-in, and how proud he must have been at the 1931 Boxing Day meet at Pewsey Market Place. From a Noah's Ark houndvan, out tumbled foxhounds and beagles in a heap, the little ones quite unconcerned and jaunty.[23] Peter hunted his hounds, while his brother Mike, home from Canada, hunted the P.V.B. Later beagles were busy at work drawing Pewsey Old Golf Course,* their young whipper-in alert and attentive, when foxhounds flashed by on their fox. Hark For'ard fails to describe hare sport, being too out of breath following Charlie up the greasy, chalk face of impossible Martinsell Hill. Lady Dulverton says there was never a dull moment that season.

Derek was to die young and never able to fulfil his promise as a huntsman. His father was devastated, and longing for quiet fishing on the Test River, he rented The Island, near Romsey, a charming house nearly surrounded by water, where wisteria covers red brick walls, to spread mauve sprays on high chimney stacks. But Henry never arrived at The Island.[24]

Hacking out one morning, his heart weakened by frequent cardiac attacks, his faltering sight did not see the danger! He fell with his horse into a wasp's nest! Both man and horse were terribly stung, and Henry never recovered, but died of shock and heart failure, aged forty-nine.[25]

**Now the Council housing estate.*

Chapter 9

Shadows then Sunshine! 1934 – 1952

Cedric Brudenell-Bruce, Earl of Cardigan, was serving on the Hunt Committee in February 1936 when Lady Wright made a verbal offer to continue hunting the country with Sir Gordon Ley, Bart.,[1] then Master of the Hursley. A generous subscriber for many years, Lady Wright had taken over the helm after Henry's resignation, and served as sole Master for one season only.

The wife of Sir Robert Alderson Wright, later Baron Wright, Privy Councillor, she was a Margery Bullows before she married in 1928, and they lived at Durley House on the southern edge of Tottenham Park.[2] A postcard of the opening meet at Durley shows Lady Wright with hounds, and like her counterpart Lady Yarrow, she rides astride dressed in black. A rather taciturn and elderly Sir Gordon, a Welshman from Penrith, appears in another photograph to have turned away from his joint Master! He brought Will James with him from the Hursley as huntsman. Lord Wright appears in several pictures as a stout gentleman wearing a bowler hat. At the Fairway, he seems to be regarding hound discipline severely; and was considered a formidable adversary in court, before he became a judge, Lord of Appeal and Master of the Rolls.[3]

Well known in every show ring in the country as a successful show jump rider, Lady Wright was full of courage. She had a serious accident in August 1933 when competing at Lambourne, and broke her pelvis. Undeterred, she was riding again the following spring. During her best year she was second in the "Daily Mail Cup" at Olympia.

Mrs. Betty Lake, who has lived at Luten Lye for thirty years, moved from Cheshire to look after Lady Wright's horses. There were twenty horses in the stables at Durley, and as there were only six boxes, many more had to be built. "She was not pretty," says Betty. "But vivacious and full of life. And very good to us girls."

Local people remember her for instructing her horse with a:

"Hip! Hip!" before each jump. Therefore it was inescapable that a happy crowd shouted:

"Hooray!"

With each cheer, Ikey's daughter Miss Diana Bell would have watched from the paddock smoking her endless cigarettes.

Loved by the crowds, Betty remembers the pageant organised by Lady Wright at Olympia as one of the half-hour shows. The "Life of John Mytton" was the theme, all the girls took part in it. From a crowded waggon Betty was dressed as an old lady throwing bouquets.

Lady Wright entered the Grand Ring dressed as the celebrated Mytton. She was driving a dogcart with two horses, a leader and a wheeler, along a road with a gate. A horse-dealer in eighteenth century costume sat beside her.

Over the loudspeakers Mytton says:

"Does this pony jump?"

"Yes, Sir. To be sure, that he does. Like a stag, to be sartin' he does."

"Hip! Hip!" orders John Mytton.

"Hooray!" roars the crowd right on cue, and the leader jumps the gate to leave the wheeler and cart behind.

Quick and resourceful always, one freezing winter day hounds were hunting the pale straw-coloured fields, flecked with snow under Martinsell Hill. A vixen, being little bigger or heavier than a large Tom cat, slithered over the great ice sheets covering the Kennet and Avon Canal near New Mill. Weed and reed ice-locked in the frozen flow hid her escape in the afternoon gloom. Hounds hunting slowly, halted in the canal-edge snow. Two couples, bolder than the rest, leaped onto the ice which, near border-mud and drift rubbish, held their weight. Halfway across the ice cracked and two of the hounds disappeared, one swam under the covering, while another pawed frantically, chipping away at edges of ice too weak to hold him.[4]

Lady Wright galloping up, dismounted, and jumped into the water, smashing at the ice with her whip, with joyful hounds scratching, scrambling and pawing to her side. Soaked and filthy, we hope the Master called it a day, and returned to Durley for a hot bath and whisky.

Small and fair, she was great fun, and the house echoed with laughter when excellent Law Lords discarded their robes to wine and dine at Durley. The following morning they would enjoy some rough shooting for rabbits in the forest-park.

Mentally counting the shots, Lady Wright worked on in her garden to restore her spirits after a heavy evening entertaining Law wives. Unlike the Scarletts she loved gardening, and the soft mist that hangs around the Forest. Being a "doggy lady", afternoons found her walking the fertile paddocks of Durley towards Forest leaf-mould paths, ways noiseless to footfall, the dogs obediently at heel. They hardly disturbed nervous deer picking hopefully at grass half-choked by bracken where ancient trees had fallen and never been re-planted. At home, venerable Lordships and their wives slept their lunch away.

Meantime, perhaps Chandos, the sixth Marquess riding through Savernake on Billy, his old charger from the First World War, felt frustrated. His financial strait-jacket meant he could employ only a dozen men to look after the Forest where a hundred were engaged by his forebears. Change was being forced upon him. Already in 1930 negotiations had been entered into with the Forestry Commission for leasing the sylvicultural rights of Savernake. However, these had failed.

But a spirit of compromise was in the air, and by 1939 an agreement to lease the Forest for nine hundred and ninety-nine years was signed with the Commissioners.[5] The hereditary Wardenship was retained by the Marquess and his heirs, so that the Tedworth Hunt was still welcome in Savernake.

Although he never hunted, a photograph shows his son Cedric, Lord

Cardigan, standing with his wife at the Fairway meet. A brilliant and charming man with dark hair and moustache, he was Chairman of the Hunt Committee from early 1938 until 1940, when W.W.2 claimed him for military duties. Commissioned to the R.A.S.C. (T.A.) he went to France, and was made a prisoner before the evacuation of Dunkirk. Escaping, he made his way to Spain where he was imprisoned by the authorities. An accomplished author,[6] his book *I Walked Alone* is an amusing record of his adventures, while *The Wardens of Savernake Forest* is a beautifully written and interesting account of the twenty-nine hereditary Wardens. A keenly observant man, we are honoured to have had him as Chairman for so many years. During the war Chandos took Cedric's chair until he returned. However, he resigned in 1946, when the Brudenell-Bruce family was represented by Lady Rosemary, a great friend of Lady Wright.

Since equestrian events are much to the fore, the *Point-to-Point Calendar* says that a "Bona Fide" Hunt and Military Meeting was held on 17 April 1937 at the Windmill Hill racecourse. The meeting was organised by the Salisbury Plain Race Club, who were our most generous subscribers.

An agreement with the Hunt signed in 1931 gave the first £50 of profit to us, together with a further four shares. One share each of the proceeds went to the promoters, who were either the Royal Artillery Harriers, 2nd Cavalry Brigade, 60th Rifles or R.A. (Salisbury Plain). As well as the lion's share of the profits, the Salisbury Plain Race Club gave the Hunt a subscription of £500, which was reviewed annually. Freddy Edmeades' name, later he was M.F.H., R.A.H. appears in the winners' list, as does Colonel Brian Thatcher, R.A.

As well as the point-to-point, the hunt ball has always been an important source of revenue, and 1938 accounts show that with tickets at twenty-five shillings, £153 profit was made.

Ashton and Mitchell's band greeted guests arriving at Sir John Kelk's porte-cochère on the north side of Tedworth House. The great Ionic columns of Mr. Assheton Smith's front door had been incorporated into the ballroom, and no longer did six foxes' masks in glass cases eye the chattering crowd in the hall. Instead, guests passed into a domed central saloon with its Victorian stained glass windows, depicting a stork or peacock set in oval medallions, and decorated with golden corn, poppy and periwinkle.

Only the dining-room survives the Kelk restoration, while gold cups and plates no longer adorned the tables, pleasant with Mrs. Drumbeck's carnations and roses. Gone too was the Duke of Wellington's statuette. His marble face did not see our friend Mr. Osmond the butcher's catering at the 1938 hunt ball! Perhaps this was the grandson of the man who rode through luggage-trolleys of Pewsey station. The traditional salmon, lobster and turkey supper was served for ten shillings a head.

Matilda Smith might have recognised crinolines in ice-blue lace trimmed with cyclamen velvet that were fashionable in Coronation year. Older ladies wore purple satin, eye-shrieking against red tailcoats.Two ten-foot mirrors reflected happy faces, unaware that gold paint was peeling from cornice and pelmet. Not being psychic, Tedworth Hunt subscribers, so long bounded in shades of Assheton Smith, did not perceive the ghost of the old Squire's nose follow the smell of mutton-hash, ladled out at the free supper for chauffeurs in the Y.M.C.A. canteen costing the organisers ninepence a portion.

It was fitting that Captain Rodney H. Palmer, 12th Lancers, later Lieutenant Colonel, M.C., M.F.H., South Berks 1947, of Fittleton Manor, took over the mastership for the last year of peace, before proceeding overseas with his regiment. He had hoped to hunt the country four days a week in conjunction with the Tedworth Woodland, but war and financial difficulties said this was not to be, while the autumn saw the deaths of both Admiral Marx and Sir Cosmo Antrobus.

Salisbury Plain was becoming overshadowed by images of war. Military training was stepped up, with a certain amount of equipment coming through that nobody had ever seen before. On 28 August 1939 Montgomery took over the 3rd Division and put everyone through it. Full mobilisation was ordered for 1st August.[7]

A last anecdote is told by Jim Read. As boys he and Peter Horton, both later Tedworth Masters, exchanged ponies, because Peter's was too strong for him, and Jim's too small. The new pony was fat and slow and hunting in a fog Jim was left behind. Now the Plain above Widdington is an eerie place at the best of times and in a mist everything appears the same, being uniform brown space, with sounds of poltergeist laughter.

Fortunately a whipper-in came along to gather up hounds, together with one frightened boy, who never really enjoyed hunting the Impact Area, ever since that foggy day!

Mr. J. C. Porter, of Sunnyhill, Honorary Secretary for so many years, now served as Acting Master until 1946. It is interesting to note how many Masters had served first on the Committee, and when their masterships ended, they continued as valuable officers. This underlines the "family" tradition of the Hunt, in its outstanding country of pastoral vale and woodland.

J. C. Porter, Esq., M.F.H., 1946-49.

"As children we were terrified of him!" writes Mr. Barry Wookey, of Upavon Manor, describing Mr. Porter. "But he was very kind to us children and often took me on point and explained what was happening. He was also a past master at spending a penny without getting off his horse!"

With no hunting Master to foot the bill, and the loss of military subscriptions, the Hunt was hard hit by the war. Hounds were reduced from thirty-one to twenty couples and later to fifteen. All poultry claims had to be waived, while keepers and earth-stoppers were asked to continue their jobs as a war effort. Only the kennelhuntsman was lucky! His wages were increased to £3 10s. a week. The remaining two horses were kindly looked after during the summer by Monty Read at Stanton St. Bernard. He loved all country sports, shooting and fishing. He also hunted with the Beaufort.

The Hunt was abandoned in 1942. Ten couple of hounds were drafted to the Wylye Valley pack, with ten couple lent to the Craven, Will James accompanying them, while seventeen were offered to officers at the experimental station, and one hates to imagine for what purpose! The single horse with his saddle and bridle were given to Will James, desolate at leaving. And all was silent. Hounds were never to return to kennels at Tedworth after over one hundred and fourteen years.

Meantime R.A. (Bulford) Harriers converted to foxhounds, to protect chickens and young lambs on the Plain.

In March 1946 with the war ended, a well-attended meeting at the Greyhound Hotel, Pewsey, decided that the horn should sound again in Pewsey Vale.

"Ways and means have to be found," said Lord Cardigan, "to put the Hunt on its feet," while Mr. Butler, the new Secretary, thought that:

"In a difficult world it is time to bring back some of the cheerful, sane and colourful things we have all missed during the past years. Hunting is especially important for young people to learn and enjoy."

Mr. Porter was now the sole Master. He was a true hunting man, who not only loved the sport, but also did an enormous amount to keep the Tedworth Hunt alive during very difficult times. He farmed at Sunnyhill, which lies under the warm, sheltered, strip-lynchets of Oare Hill. He was also a lawyer, being a partner in Messrs. Merriman, Porter and Young, of Marlborough. Perhaps his legal mind made him so terrifying to Barry Wookey!

Terrifying or not, he drafted a most generous agreement with the Hunt to lodge hounds at Sunnyhill, because the kennels roof at Tedworth, a sore for so many years, was beyond repair. Besides Mr. Porter, as the new Master, wanted his hounds under his solicitous eye.

SUNNYHILL

Per annum	
Huntsman's house at 12/6d per week (Council House basis)	£32
3 Loose boxes and saddle room —say	£5
Interest on £300, my capital expenditure on kennels and converting 3 loose boxes, at 3% + depreciation at 1%—4%	£12
Repairs, rates and taxes, insurance and electric light in respect of all the above items—say	1
	£61

But say £50 per annum

NOTE: Rates and taxes to be mutually adjusted in the event of re-assessment as non-agricultural premises or if substantially increased on quinquennial re-valuation.

Kennels and huntsman's house are situated to the west of Sunnyhill Farm, and on the same side of the road leading to Milkhouse Water. Above them is the wind-protecting escarpment of Oare and Martinsell Hills, topped by Tan Hill Way, where Jack Fricker hunted Assheton Smith's great hounds. The farmhouse itself is built of brick with a dark, glazed, geometric pattern to give it lightness, which is such a feature of the south Wiltshire/Hampshire border houses. A tiled roof has tall, thick chimney stacks, and envelops Sunnyhill like a blanket, to enfold odd bays with sash windows. French doors open below small panes of glass, leading to an assortment of built-on wings and outshuts and hips, until it resembles a red Hobbit-demesne. It is a topsy sort of place, that grew from cottages to farm. Across warm south pasture the London train hoots as it passes Pewsey station, to follow the Avon and Kennet Canal eastwards towards Newbury.

Draft hounds had to be found and twenty-six packs were approached before Will James, who returned from the Craven, could start to educate young hounds in Glass Wood rented for fourteen seasons by Mr. Porter. On 2 November, he might have been seen leading sixteen couples of very assorted hounds towards Stowell crossroads. At the opening meet a mounted field of almost pre-war dimensions, including farmers from the Avon Vale, met the gratified Master. There were so many people on foot that it might have been a Boxing Day celebration.

A photograph shows Mr. Porter riding his white horse, Dawn. Lady Ernest St. Maur, who always had a fox in Wilcot withybed, was there as she continued to ride to hounds until she was seventy-five. Bob House, of Pewsey, nicknamed "Boadicea", as being too crippled with arthritis to ride, he drove his two-wheeled milk-float down the road to watch James draw Stowell Park, which always held plenty of foxes. Hounds hunted round the park which surrounds the handsome Georgian house, where wisteria clings to a white wrought-iron loggia. Then off through beech trees and box towards the meadow in front of Park Copse, where several horses, being unused to hunting, made heavy weather of post-and-rails, to the chagrin of riders. The tally was two sets of broken ribs!

"At Draycot Farm Charlie was given up," writes Hark For'ard. "Hounds were not a particularly level lot, but handsome is as handsome does, and they put up a good performance from Lady Ernest's withybeds, where a leash was soon on foot. Settling on a line to Woodborough Hill, they circled right-handed and drove him towards Alton Priors. Then galloping over the White Horse at racing pace, they marked their fox to ground at Milk Hill, after a point of five miles in seventy minutes."

Mr. Barry Wookey remembers that, "After the war, when I started hunting again, Mr. Porter asked why I wasn't out 'last Saturday'. When I suggested that it may have been because it was pouring with rain, he took a dim view and said I 'would never be a true hunting man'. He himself was just that, a true hunting man who not only loved the sport but also did an enormous amount to keep the Tedworth Hunt alive during very difficult times."

1947-48 was a critical year for the Tedworth, with the first seeds of dispute surfacing with the R.A. (Salisbury Plain) foxhounds over hunting territory. Captain Thorne, a short, stocky, determined man assured the January '49 meeting that he was keeping the spirit of foxhunting alive in the south of the country. Some members were dubious. They wondered how much country? And for how long? Already several meets had clashed.

That same year a written agreement was signed between Mr. Butler and Brigadier J. H. Gibbon, D.S.O., Chairman of the R.A.H. (see Appendix). Such parts not included in the schedule were to be regarded by the R.A. (S.P.) Hunt as "neighbouring country". This area applied to Bulford Ranges.

This was Mr. Porter's last year as he resigned in 1950, after twenty-five years as a friend of the Hunt and eleven as Master. Presenting him with an inscribed silver salver, and his wife with a cocktail set, Mr. Butler said:

"After the war, we had no staff, no kennels, no hounds, no stabling and no accommodation. Mr. Porter provided them all!"

He was the saviour of the Hunt.

Mr. Philip Dunn was the next joint Master with the Earl of Hardwicke. They were tremendous friends, and it appears likely that Hardwicke came to the Tedworth at Dunn's instigation. Also the Hunt was desperate to find Masters able to contribute to the expense of the pack.

The flamboyant ninth Earl lived at Rockley Manor, a house he bought north-west of Marlborough, near Manton Down. Rockley is remembered as the home of generous Hugh de Heinz Whatton, and is a very ancient manor listed in the Domesday book. Square, white, with a slate roof, it stands quiet and serene in a sheltered valley.[8] This is Vine and Craven country, but when Hardwicke was Master, hounds enjoyed several cub-hunting mornings from Rockley.

The pack would have been led by George Goodwin, who came to us from the Woodland Pychley. Hounds crossed the lawn towards the ha-ha in front of a handsome portico which stands at right angles to a No Through Road. Obedient, sensitive, as animals are, feeling the last wish of Hugh Whatton on the breath of grass, they sat in a tight huddle. The bitches whined softly, understanding Hugh's longing to be buried at St. Catherine's Chapel, Savernake, because the ha-ha and trees recalled beloved Rockley.

The Earl of Hardwicke, M.F.H., 1949-54. Photograph of painting by Poret reproduced by kind permission of his daughter, Lady Amabel Lindsay.

The horn blew, and they set off past the cramped school, now an antique restorer's workshop. Then they skirted a minute chapel, where the bell once tolled the faithful to repentance, and today calls babies and infants to their crèche.

The Earl, riding as field Master, was Gloucestershire born and educated at Eton and Sandhurst. A strong, bluff man and full of fun, he became an officer with the Life Guards, and flew with the Army Air Corps. Later he was a Major with the Royal Artillery, while in W.W.2 he served with the First Airborne Division.[9]

"I liked him," says Jim Read. "He was pleasant."

A tall, red-faced, well set-up man weighing about fifteen stone, he rode large horses. However, the Earl, known as the "puffing peer", could be somewhat overpowering towards young ladies such as Barbara Read, who was new to the hunting field!

Now as a bride Barbara hunted for a short time, before the children came along, and her life became too busy.

One day hounds were running her father-in-law's land near Stanton St. Bernard, and a little uncertain, she rode tight behind the Earl as field Master. Suddenly his horse gave Barbara's mare a vicious kick! She was devastated.

"You were riding too close," he said, turning away. "You shouldn't ride so close."

A complete contrast in character was his joint Master, Gordon Philip Dunn. He later became Sir Philip Dunn, second baronet (U.K.), of Bathurst, Province of New Brunswick, and lived at Stowell Park[10] with its wisteria, where coverts are a habitat of foxes. A Canadian, Dunn had financial interests in Algoma Steel. He was a quiet, charming man, and a very good rider but, being shy, some people thought him difficult! An undeserved comment!

Mr. Dunn bought the farm at the Park together with one hundred and twenty-six acres. Mr. John Wallis, land agent for the estate since 1958, describes how gradually farms at East and West Stowell, also Draycot, were added so that today Stowell Park comprises fifteen hundred acres.

When Philip Dunn first came, Kennet country was very different compared with today. A hutted Army camp built during the war stood at Alton Barnes crossroads, and each morning a lorry transported soldiers to the concrete military road built on Read farmland at West Kennet. A red flag was flown. Then when the hooter sounded, shells were fired on the testing range, active until 1960. On spring evenings at dusk, as the transport brought soldiers home to tea in the cookhouse, the road became alive with rabbits. The Downs appeared to heave and shudder, so that hunting was treacherous with rabbit-holes.

Wiltshire War Agricultural Committee, No. 2 District.
L to R (back row): A. J. D. Lavis, L. Leyton, G. A. Young, O. M. Peall, W. J. Brimacombe, J. B. Wroth, W. E. T. Lock, W. J. Osmond.
(Front row): A. B. Kerr, E. B. Gauntlett, C. P. Wookey (Chairman), F. Swanton, T. G. Blanchard.

However, when Philip Dunn first became Master, it was possible to go to Fosbury, then 3,500 acres, and the adjoining land which in the 'fifties was not heavily shot at any time. Therefore the Hunt used to rely on this Tuesday country which included Biddesden, Collingbourne and Savernake. In the last thirty-five years there has been a complete change of emphasis in the hunting country, so that now we have to rely on Stowell/Read country.

Under this mastership the pack was brought up to about thirty couple, and two days and a bye were hunted, with the supply of foxes much improved. The Committee hoped these two Masters would get the Tedworth back to something like its original glories. With the advent of a chemical lavatory at kennels for the use of whipper-in and kennelman, things were looking up. Mr. Yorke Scarlett was still going strong. And the meeting in August was closed to the accompaniment of a violent thunderstorm.

Things did not always run smoothly. Apparently a lady who lived in

Milton Lilbourne complained that hounds had disturbed her sheep. Also that in January they had damaged bulbs in the garden. An amusing letter from Lord Hardwicke strongly refutes her accusations.

He knew she had lambing ewes in her paddock. Therefore, when drawing Mr. Porter's gorse, he spread the field out across the kennel paddock from the yard towards Sunnyhill, to head the fox if he broke towards her land. Unfortunately the fox doubled back and took a line down the side of the hedgerow near the lady's Guernsey cattle. But he says:

"Hounds were never in the same field as your sheep!"

As for the garden bulbs he points out that hounds have not only been across his own flower-beds at Rockley, but have broken up a fox when bulbs were much further advanced. A few days later there was no trace of damage.

Unfortunately, Philip Dunn resigned at the end of 1950-51 season, leaving Hardwicke as the forceful, sole Master.

The following season hounds were hunting Boreham Wood, and Lady Rosemary Brudenell-Bruce was whipping-in. At three o'clock, as it was growing dusk, Jim Read said:

"George isn't going to find a fox now."

"Goodwin! Not find a fox!" said Hardwicke. "We'll see about that."

"You can see George wants to go home. He won't find another."

"We're not going home until we find another fox. George! D'you hear?" Sure enough soon after that another fox was found and they had a good run.

However, Hardwicke had never hunted the pack himself and did not know if hounds were hunting hare, deer or fox, while George, being a natural scallywag, liked to keep his Master happy. Major Ashton remembers wonderful runs from Everleigh to Tidworth, when they never stopped galloping all day. Hound-jogging home, Charles Ashton rode up alongside Goodwin.

"George," said the Major, who was a keen beagler. "Pity you were hunting hare, not fox!" George said nothing because he was often a difficult, morose man.

Today, looking northwards from Stowell Park and thinking of Philip Dunn, thousands of acres of wheat or barley, like a fertile sea, shelter under the steep protecting bays of Draycot Hill, Golden Hill and Knap Camp. The colours of the escarpment are peach and indigo where sheep graze, looking like white pincushions on a wall. Since the rabbit clearances this is good galloping country. There are no shoots, there never have been. No pheasants, no wire and no keepers. To the north of the road, land farmed by the Stratton family for over a hundred years, and now by Mr. Tim Carson, Mr. Guy Stratton's grandson, separates Stowell Park estates from Read land at Stanton St. Bernard.

The Earl of Hardwicke must have been reluctant to leave this interesting hunting country when he resigned in 1954.

Chapter 10

"Better than the Fireside"

"He was marvellous," says Lady Moyne. "Monty was a wonderful man!"

People said he had a twinkle, so that you never knew if he were being serious.

"One day when we were out hunting, it was pouring with rain," she goes on. "It was coming down in sheets. The wind was blowing, and it was raining so hard, that you couldn't see anything. Monty riding alongside said: 'Well! This is better than sitting by the fireside'!"

Monty Read was Master 1954-58, then joint Master with Sir Philip Dunn 1958-64. The Read family originally came from Downton, where they were tenants of Lord Radnor, owner of romantic Longford Castle. As a very young man Monty was apprenticed to a corn merchant at Warminster, and he often visited Imber before the Army pounded it to rubble. In those days, Imber Court was a lovely house rebuilt for Sir Henry Holloway's estate manager Major Whistler. You could drive to church along an avenue of lime trees, and there were five tennis courts in the village. Of special interest to Monty Read, would have been the big shoots for partridge, hare, pheasants, rabbit or woodcock.

In 1921 he moved to Church Farm, Stanton St. Bernard as a tenant farmer on Lord Pembroke's estate, where he rode everywhere and spoke to everyone. Records first mention him as an energetic member of the Hunt Committee, but greyhounds were his greatest love. When we meet foxhounds at Stanton and cross the Devizes to Pewsey road, then trot northwards along the trackway leading to Milk Hill, we pass the evocative Dogrun field, where Monty used to race his greyhounds. The hares were let out by the barn, and then bolted to Dogrun Covert. Once there were two nut bushes spaced out for coursing, but the nut spinney is today chocked with alder.

Monty was one of the first men to race at the White City, and probably served on the original committee. His grandson Bryan remembers pictures of greyhounds on Church farmhouse walls. There were no foxes' masks, and just a brush or two, but dozens of greyhound photographs. Pigeon racing was another fancy, together with partridge shooting at Stanton and East Kennet. He also had a pheasant shoot at Cowdown Farm, near Andover, and Monty hunted two days a week with the Beaufort.

His wife never hunted. She was the daughter of Henry Sawtell, feather purifier of Melksham, and while raising their family the farm grew and prospered. They were able to buy two and a half thousand acres of arable and dairy pastures, with sheep folded on the cold, chalk upland rising to the north of their land. Monty managed the farm himself with a foreman, while Jack Young of Huish was manager of the East Kennet side.

One of the early memories of his son Jim, elected to the Hunt Committee in 1955, was of sacks of oats being prepared in his father's farmyard ready for Tedworth kennels. Monty and other farmers in those days provided hay, straw and oats for the Hunt, and Jim's father co-ordinated and collected contributions. As the waggons were loaded, teams of horses could look south across the meadows towards the canal, where up to four hundred Friesian cows grazed, their milk cooled and processed in five dairies belonging to the farm.

Horses and waggons pulled alongside farm-buildings, some of which are now converted or rebuilt into the riding-school, and drove down the tree-lined drive. Pigeons flew from a loft in a granary wall. Monty's hunters were kept in five stables at the back of the substantial brick and slate farmhouse. In the depression he hunted six days a week.

Monty had been joint Master during the 1953-54 season, but on the resignation of both the Earl of Hardwicke and Philip Dunn, his offer to hunt the country for a guarantee of £2000 was accepted with gratitude. A picture of the new Master in the *Wiltshire Gazette* shows a spare, athletic man with glasses. He was quiet, reserved, and to his grandchildren, a little aloof. To match a soft Wiltshire accent, there was that wonderful smile of his. He was a countryman who worked on the land and loved it with an unselfconscious pride.

Monty Read Esq., M.F.H. 1952-64, at meet of Tedworth foxhounds outside Castle and Ball Hotel, Marlborough.

At the annual meeting in the Savernake Forest Hotel, the chairman Mr. Butler said:

"I think in these days to keep this old, quiet, leisurely country sport of foxhunting going is well worth while." He spoke of the puppy show, and felt that hounds were getting better each year. George Goodwin had obtained a post in Warwickshire, so Len Lloyd, who arrived in 1953 from the North Warwickshire, was huntsman, and he always brought out the useful pack in tip-top form. After the meeting there was a cocktail party when one hundred people turned up.

That autumn luck was not on the side of the new mastership. Weather was atrocious and the harvest a month late, making cub-hunting impossible. The next annual meeting brought calls for more hunting on Salisbury Plain.

"We have been there a good few times lately," replied Mr. Read, smiling that smile when nobody knew if he were serious or no. "Then a lot of people grumble. And each time my skin gets thicker! I do the best I can, and if I upset owners and keepers, then I am worse off. Several times you ask me *not* to go there. And I haven't gone!" And he smiled, which goes to show a person could take Monty both ways!

The Master did a great deal to help Hunt finances. He persuaded Morris Nicol and the Pewsey people to hold a Hunt sale, and also he organised the first moonlight steeplechase.

The great excitement of 1955 was a subsequent moonlight steeplechase at beautiful Rainscombe Park. During the loveliest of summers, rays from a July moon, rising above Martinsell Hill, homed-in on three marquees, pale against park trees of Rainscombe House. The moonbeams hitting white canvas in the epicentre of a natural dell, appeared to reinforce sound waves from the dance band, until music and light resonated from the upturned bell of surrounding hills.

Inside the tent, Tommy Kinsman's band would have played *Magic Moments* because it was the hit of the year, besides they were enchanted by the place, the flowers and the gardens. Some of the girls wore fashionable, short, lampshade frocks, while mothers clung to long gowns.

Outside was heard the familiar sound of horseboxes turning on gravel. However horses were uncertain when off-loaded in the dark, with girl jockeys giggling at the prospect of upsidedown bridles, while pints of beer on trestle-tables assisted left-hand spurs to be attached to right boots. The races were dominated by women, while the men did the important course-building and stewarding, also rescued fallers from amongst the eleven starters in the first race. Jesamine, belonging to our hostess, Mrs. H. P. Drewry, and ridden by Miss E. A. Perkins, won for the third year running. Miss Belinda Stent came in second on her own Gypsy, with Mrs. J. Salmond on Sankey.

Dancing on a summer night continued amongst floral decorations, with the band *Sing'in' the Rain,* and remembering *When Somebody thinks You're Wonderful,* in good London dance orchestra fashion. Donald Sinden, of Arthur Rank and T.V. fame, danced with his hostess. Hunting stories were exchanged in the bar, with Mr. Morris Nicol giving ungrudging help, while cooks lit Calor-gas burners for breakfast.

Thirteen entries faced the starter for the second race, with down-air cooling the dew, to make ladies shiver. Hilary Watts rode Joe Howse's Flick to win. Cool Mist, ridden by Miss C. Kendall, came second, with young George Drewry, the only chap to gain honours, riding Lady Wright's Buckingham.

A procession of storm-lanters brought winners to the front of the marquee, where Donald Sinden presented prizes kindly given by Mrs. Drewy. Then lady jockeys metamorphosed into butterflies, and after sausage, steak, bacon and eggs, dancing continued until Saturday morning. We do not know if in the early hours the band played the new Elvis Presley *Heartbreak Hotel,* to the intense delight of a fledgling *Rock 'n' Roll* generation.

Lady Wright, perhaps recalling pageants at Olympia, and hearing the incomprehensible nuances of *Heartbreak Hotel,* must have felt desolate that Mrs. Porter was no longer in the marquee to sit with her. Listening to the impetuous beat, a chill wind rose as the moon set. Mrs. Porter had died the previous year, and her goodly fellowship was a pleasure lost to all her friends. Also her death had unfortunate repercussions, as Mr. Porter decided to sell Sunnyhill, and the sale included kennels, which made hounds and horses feel uncertain of their fate.

At first it appeared that all might be well. Mr. Oscar Peall, a member of the Committee, was the new owner. A satisfactory if more expensive agreement was reached, and with history repeating itself, repairs were made to the lodging-house roof. Then Peall suddenly changed his mind, and gave the Hunt notice to quit kennels! Apparently he needed the cottage which was tenanted by the whipper-in. The Committee was furious, and a sub-committee was formed to search for new premises, but it was not until the following year that Westcourt, near Burbage, was purchased, and after the sale of Sunnyhill, on 12 October 1957, hounds and horses had a permanent home of their own.

Westcourt is in a small hamlet north-west of Burbage on a small bye-road, and the property was bought for £4,250. To meet the purchase price, shares in fifty pound units at three per cent were issued, and twenty-eight shares were bought on the first day. Colonel Kidston-Montgomerie put up the £3000 of the purchase price in shares which were re-distributed in the 1970's as he felt it wrong for his estate to hold such a large percentage should he die. (He died in 1993.) The original purchases of the balance were families who bought in the names of their children or grandchildren, many of whom still hold them. The kennel committee in 1957 included Mr. J. C. Porter, Lieutenant Colonel E. W. Oxenford and Mr. Morris Nicol.

Len Lloyd, leading the pack towards Westcourt for the first time, must have felt deep satisfaction. Was it he who painted *T. H. Kennels* on the green gable above the centre line of boxes? He had laboured for endless hours to transform the original racing stables into lodges suitable for hounds, and so saved the Hunt a great deal of expense. A short, dapper man he was very keen and reliable and always hunted hounds for the Masters.

The three sides of the quadrangle stands behind an attractive, red brick, slated house with six bays. Its iron garden railings seem to have escaped the scrapman's shears during the last war. Mr. Swanson, of Park Farm, Clench Common, lived here as a boy. His father used Westcourt to breed greyhounds, who were lodged in boxes once constructed for racehorses. There was a greyhound racing track leading from the gardens round the outside perimeter to the back of the stables. Nowadays at Park Farm Mr. Swanson enjoys driving Welsh ponies on carriage driving competitions.

There are twelve boxes in the yard with interconnecting doors. All are metal-lined and steel-braced, although they seem rather deep and narrow. Perhaps they held thin thoroughbreds! Kennels stand at right angles to the main section, and dogs and bitches are lodged together, with whelping boxes next to them.

A fascinating asbestos pipe sprouts out of the wall below *T. H. Kennels*. This led from a tortoise stove used to heat the tack room. There was also a boiler where pudding was prepared for hounds and fed to them each day using oats supplied by the Hortons, Reads, Wookeys and Swantons, together with vegetables, meat and broth. An archway by the tackroom is the entrance to modern skinning rooms and deep freezes. The entire establishment comprises about three acres, and there are two paddocks for horses, and a grass yard for hounds to stretch and play.

Lady Dulverton writes that in Philip Dunn's time when he was attempting to build up a moderate pack she was approached for drafts, but having given up the North Cotswold she could be of little help. However, she put the Masters in touch with Captain Wallace of the Heythrop, and the Duke of Beaufort gave them some stallion hounds. She also asked the great breeder Sir Newton Ryecroft with his wonderful Welsh blood. Peter Farquhar and Monty Read got on tremendously well together.

The 1946-49 F.K.S.Bs show that the new entry was entirely composed of draft hounds. South and West Wilts blood appears strongly, together with W.V.H. (Lord Bathurst's), the West Dulverton and Avon Vale, also other notable packs. In 1950 only two puppies were out of a Tedworth bitch, similarly in 1951, with a preponderance of drafts from the Portman, Beaufort, Avon Vale and South and West Wilts.

However, by 1952 ten of the nineteen puppies entered were out of Tedworth bitches, although 1953 shows all drafts particularly from the Beaufort and Avon Vale. It is not until 1954 that all entries by the kennel committee were Tedworth bred.

At the annual meeting, the Chairman, Lieutenant Colonel G. J. Kidston-Montgomerie, thanked Len Lloyd for the work he had done at Westcourt House.

"He has worked like a navvy and done a lot more than a huntsman could be expected to do. Now we have the finest kennels and the best pack of hounds we have had for a long time. As to the future I can never say it is rosy financially because we are digging into reserves."

In 1959 there was general satisfaction when Sir Philip Dunn, home from business in Canada, came to the rescue to join Monty as joint Master. He was very generous towards the Hunt, although being a private, very reserved man, when a large field came out for one of the more popular meets, he was known to say:

"We've got enough out! I'd rather put a bit more money in than have more out!"

Collingbourne Woods were made available to the Tedworth through the generosity of Mr. Yorke Scarlett. They were re-negotiated after his death by Colonel Kidston-Montgomerie.* And 1933 had seen the re-planting of the forest which had been creamed-off of large trees during the Great War. Conifers, planted in regimental ranks, stood higher than riders' heads when Len Lloyd cheered on hounds, to penetrate bramble and the tangled undergrowth of Collingbourne. The tree-canopy had not grown sufficiently by 1960 to keep the forest floor clean of creeper as it is today.

Eric Waldron, whipping-in to Len, was having a miserable day, because his Irish mount, a big, black horse with a white face named Lightning, was pulling his arms out. The gelding was all sweated up with specks of blood about his mouth. Sir Philip spoke to Len:

"Before you draw again, I would like to try that horse."

However, Len was not so sure. "Sir," he whispered to Jim Read, "stay with him. He's a small man, and we cannot afford to lose him. He'll get run away with. Master's too precious."

"You know," says Jim. "That horse never pulled a bit. Dunn rode him for years. Never had any trouble. He'd go first or last. Wonderful hands had Sir Philip!" And Jim ought to know.

In racing towards modern times we must not forget that Willie Yorke Scarlett died in 1956, and few remain these days to carry on a tradition of loyalty and generosity enshrined in old-world courtesy. Only a small photograph records the lovely presentation picture painted of the Godfather and Charlie, both mounted and with hounds in a favourite sun-filled combe, perhaps near his favourite Collingbourne Woods. Another picture painted by Miss B. Shiffner lets us remember Atlas, Archer, Charmer, Tarquin, Alfred and Tarmac, whilst a third is a quite exquisite study of the pack in open, hilly terrain, reminiscent of the vales and hills of our country. The Tedworth Woodland was one of the last truly private packs.

How Mr. Yorke Scarlett might have viewed Major K. Malcolm's letter to the Hunt in October 1960 would have been unprintable! The Godfather could have dropped his monocle in a rage. Savernake of all places. No hunting until after Christmas. Unthinkable. And what would the Duke of Beaufort say?

Apparently Malcolm, recently moving from Fleet, Hampshire, to Upton, Andover, had acquired the shooting rights on Crown Lands, leased through the Marquess of Ailesbury, and bounded by Marlborough, Savernake and Clench Common. He wrote in his letter that he was refusing permission for the country to be hunted before Christmas, owing to the difficulty of retaining the expensively reared birds on the shoot in the scanty cover available.

Monty and Jim, with experience at Cowdown Farm, were of the opinion that letting hounds draw a day or two before a shoot did no harm at all, and helped to put birds up. However, Brigadier Walch had to use all his tact when he met Major Malcolm. But there was deadlock. Finally it was agreed

**Sporting rights were leased in May 1964 for seven years at annual rent and rates of £350.*

that for the 1960-61 season only, hounds would not open in Savernake until the New Year. Trouble brewed again the next season when Malcolm, an unpredictable man, suddenly withdrew permission the day before a meet, having previously agreed to dates on a friendly basis.

Tempers flared, only cooled by frost and snow, which was complicated by January lambs gambolling over snow-tipped grass-tufts on Clench Common, and playing king-of-the-castle on frozen lumps in the Forest, during one of the most frost-locked winters on record.

Perhaps tenant farmers, who were good hunting people, took a hand, Savernake being regarded as our best country, because in 1963 hounds met to draw Malcolm's kale. Kale planted as an extension to warm sheltered coverts is attractive to pheasants, as well as to a fox, their chief predator. When Lloyd put the pack in, a dozen strong, fast running birds, alarmed at being driven by hounds, raced for the edge of the kale. Then with a burst of power they rocketed from the ground in one explosive burst of adrenalin-powered energy to roost on high branches of the few mature trees. Meantime the pack was interested, with the smaller bitches leaping up to catch breast-high scent and report that Charlie was near. The fox, believing that keepers and guns were a worthwhile hazard for a night-time dinner, felt hounds to be an unnecessary risk, and made a fast escape to the catch-me-if-you-can fields and copses of the Savernake Outliers.

Troubles are inclined to attack in pairs. Amesbury Abbey, where the Antrobus family had welcomed us for a hundred and twenty years, was debarred to the Hunt by Army orders. No longer might a fox be found in the osier beds, while horsemen galloped beside the chinoiserie trellis of the verandah bridge. Sir Edmund suggested writing to the old warhorse Sir Evelyn Wood, who said that cavalry officers were made on the hunting field. But the venerable Field Marshal's views were two wars too late.

From a meet at Stowell, the most fantastic hunt of the season took place after hounds had been hunting all the morning from Wilcot and over the Downs, with its short grasses covering the ancient Long Barrows above East Kennet. Returning to the meet at three o'clock, Monty was tired, and so was his horse, therefore Jim was told to take charge as field Master.

The pack was taken to Wilcot withybeds where they put up a huge dog fox. He broke cover with hounds about fifty yards behind him. Our pilot crossed the canal and headed towards Tawsmead, then down to the corner of Workway Drove. Hounds raced over Langdons Flat only a hundred yards behind, past Shaw Farm dairy, and to the edge of Boreham Wood. The fox crossed the road and headed for Kennet but turning back made for the bottom corner of West Woods. Skirting the covert he ran to the back of Lockeridge, and down into Clatford Bottom. By this time only Jim Read, John Wallis, Barry Wookey, Peter Horton, Hilary Watts and Jack Mayell were with them, and had been galloping flat out for ninety minutes.

It was getting very dark. Hounds went over the top towards Manton, so the field split up into parties to try to stop them. Meantime Peter's horse put two feet into a badger hole, and he went down as though he were shot! Eventually hounds were caught up on the athletic track of Marlborough College. Then they had the terrible task of hacking the pack along the road in the dark, with Jim waving a white handkerchief.

Arriving in the yard at Stowell, Len arrived in his truck, having been looking for them for hours. In his Welsh way he chided:

"Look you. An' what 'av you been doing with my hounds, then?"

It was a wonderful day. One of the hunts to remember for ever.

Sir Philip Dunn divided the country into districts each with a Committee member to look after it, so that all areas could be hunted regularly every four to six weeks. Jim Read cared for Kennet, and John Wallis for Stowell, while Tom Curnick, owner of Conygre Farm and the Crown tenant of Bowden's Farm, undertook the Pewsey to Burbage area, regarded as our best parcel of land. Then Barry Wookey and Peter Horton did the Upavon, Widdington, Wilsford and Puckshipton countries, and jumps were handled by Jim Read and the stalwart Morris Nicol. Both brought another man each. Bill Boddington, one of Nicol's tent peg men, was a big fellow who drove stakes in as though they were nails! John Wallis, combining forces with Jim Read and Nicol to deal with the Stowell area, recalls that they built nine jumps in one day, and the work nearly killed him. Mr. Butler was reputed to have erected 'a thousand jumps' in Pewsey Vale, including those tiger-traps that resemble hen-coops. If you turn them upside-down while jumping, you leave a problem for the next rider.

On the social side, the barn dance at Stanton St. Bernard was one of the most popular events of the year, especially to the young of the farming community. A great number of farmers hunted. They used one horse in the morning to supervise their farms, then rode hunters in the afternoon.

The barn dance was often held in the Read's present grain-drier house, which stands where the chalk trackway from Milk Hill meets the Devizes to Alton Barnes road, and a week before the dance, Roger Upton's little car was seen parked by the thornbushes. Sounds of hammering and nailing amidst laughter came from within, while men carried fabricated timber sheets harvested from ex-Army sheds through the doorway. Morris Nicol was constructing a dance floor. Meanwhile Roger, a large tray of spray cans filled with bright orange, green, blue, red and white paint, was decorating the tin-asbestos lined walls with caricatures of subscribers to the Hunt. Nobody was safe! Horses were depicted stopping at jumps, their riders deposited head first in the mud. The cut of coats, and the height of hats were all happily lampooned. Tickets cost fifty pence, and the local Pewsey band played in the hot, steamy atmosphere. Sometimes an entertainer was hired.

Perhaps Monty stood in the cool of the night on the chalk road which leads up to his beloved Dogrun Covert. Adge Cutler and the *Wurzels* were hammering out one of their insistent Somerset songs:

"I've got a brand-new combine harvester

An' I'll giv' you the key . . . . ."

He stood there quietly, recalling his forty seven years with the Hunt. The music had stopped and the entertainer, microphone in hand, was shouting out his routine to waves of laughter. The Master listened intently, while a friend came out for a breath of cool air.

"You know," said Mr. Read, "I don't think they should tell blue jokes like that in front of ladies!"

During these years the controversy over hunting country between the Army authorities and the Tedworth Hunt was escalating. The R.A.H. was warned that owing to the general shortage of foxes it was very unlikely that the Tedworth would be able to continue invitations to hunt any country not officially loaned to them. This would apply to the Fittleton, North Tidworth, Shipton Bellinger, Crossbelt and Bulford village areas. However, owing to Sir Philip's absence abroad detailed agreement with the R.A. (S.P.) had to be held over.

By May 1964 the Committee decided that a strong line must be taken with the Army authorities to maintain the rights of the Tedworth to control the whole of their country, including War Department land. The matter was referred to G.O.C. in C. Southern Command, and later to the M.F.H.A. for a decision.

The entire problem was being exacerbated by an unexpected decision of the Beaufort Hunt to take back country loaned to the Avon Vale. This meant that Avon Vale country hunted by us had to be relinquished. Further difficulties arose due to a change of mastership.

As though to presage controversy *The Marlborough Times* printed its headlines in great black letters five-eighths of an inch high:

"TEDWORTH HUNT

SAYS FAREWELL TO RETIRING MASTERS."

Lieutenant Colonel G. J. Kidston-Montgomerie, presenting gifts of silver salvers and books, said to Mr. Read: "You have carried on in a most cheerful and happy atmosphere and made hunting with the Tedworth great fun. That great huntsman the Duke of Beaufort said to me the other day that you are all going to miss Monty.

Tedworth Hunt. Presentation to retiring joint Masters.
L to R: Sir Philip Dunn, Lieutenant Colonel G. J. Kidston-Montgomerie, Monty Read, Esq.

Sir Philip has been Master for eight happy seasons. If it had not been for you coming to the rescue on two occasions, I am sure the Tedworth would have nearly finished."

Four advertisements in *Horse and Hound* resulted in five applications being refused as unsuitable. Later an offer from the ubiquitous Mr. A. W. H. Dalgety, his friend Mrs. George Jonas, and son Mr. Hugh Dalgety was accepted. Len Lloyd was to continue as huntsman, with not less than thirty couple of hounds in kennels.

Mr. Arthur Dalgety, who had very strong opinions on hound breeding, came to us after a long and colourful career. The Hursley was closing down due to loss of hunting country. Previously Mr. Dalgety had been Master of the Dunston Harriers, the Vine and Southdown Foxhounds, and joint Master with Sir John Buchanan-Jardine of the New Forest Buckhounds, and was a much respected Master. He was related to the Australian Dalgety family who are very big stock and station agents, and operate enormous holdings in New South Wales and other states.

Dalgety was energetic and generous. Westcourt kennels were in a sad state of repair so he spent a great deal of his own money on improvements. However, Tedworth subscribers enjoying cub-hunting on autumn mornings in the 1964-65 season were amazed to see the three new Masters riding ponies! When a jump had to be taken, they dismounted, scrambled over and free-jumped their mounts. Mr. Dalgety always carried an axe on his saddle to trim awkward branches.

He was a charming, sophisticated man on his feet. But riding a horse he became very bad-tempered, and upset numerous people. From the very start things did not go well. There were mutterings and murmurings, and dissatisfaction with hunting. As early as 30 November 1964, there were calls for the Masters to be asked to resign. Part of the problem appeared to have been that Arthur Dalgety was a very old-fashioned Master. He expected his Secretary to arrange meets, and took no notice if people said he could not come to hunt.

However, very graciously the joint Masters resigned in January 1965, with Arthur Dalgety thanking the Committee for the help he had been given.

Six weeks later it was agreed unanimously to accept the offer of Mr. J. M. Read to take over the Mastership.

Chapter 11

Recollections!

"My first recollection of hunting with the Tedworth," said Mr. Jim Read, Master 1965-72, "was of two ponies, both roan. My sister Bunty* had a fat little pony, and hounds were drawing between Shaw Farm and Kennet, up on the top there."

As he reminisced we sat on cushioned, Windsor chairs at an oak refectory table in the quiet, pristine kitchen of Jim's new Swedish Scandia-Hus at Stanton St. Bernard. The cream walls above pine panelling looked homely, although he knows sadness.

"Mrs. Stratton," he went on, "had gone on point by the covert there, which must have been two or three years old. Leaves were just showing, and there was a lot of dried grass making it a wonderful fox covert. They killed, and my sister and I were blooded, so we rode back to Stanton very proud of ourselves. And it was a great trouble mother had to get us to wash it off our faces!

"We hunted with the Tedworth whenever we could, mostly cub-hunting. I was about eight and Bunty must have been ten. We went up to Savernake Forest hunting, when the meet was at Savernake hospital. We rode from Stanton on our ponies with father on his horse, and met hounds where the car park is now. That was a field at the time. After hunting with them for some hours we hacked back to Church Farm, arriving at about four o'clock. Mother was very cross because when we got off the ponies we had a job to walk up the cobbled path, we were so stiff. She took us in and gave us a hot bath, more or less putting us to bed to rest. Father got into dreadful trouble!

"The next time we went out, we hired a lorry to hunt with Captain Vigors and the Tedworth Woodland. I remember Yorke Scarlett very well. It was possible to do much more cub-hunting than it is now because the harvest was all done by horse and cart. There were no combine-harvesters, and once the corn was cut and put into riles, you could hunt between the riles and do no harm whatsoever. Also most hunts went on until they killed a May fox.

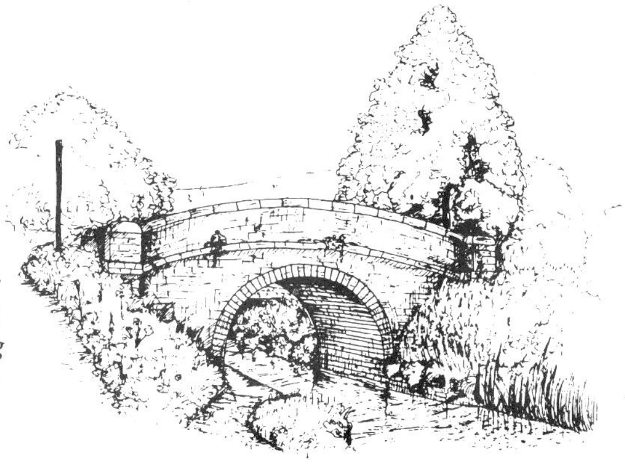

"England's Bridge" over the Kennet and Avon Canal, passing through land owned by the Read family.

*Later Mrs. Leyland-Smith.

"There were a lot of sheep about but they were in hurdles. The flocks were put out on the Downs and watched over by a shepherd and his dog. He'd call them up together if the hounds came by, so there was no problem hunting with them."

An oversize grandfather clock from Devon & Somerset Staghound country dwarfs the wall. The new house, built in the grounds of Church Farm where Jim was born, looks out over a rockery gaudy with brilliant spring heather. The vegetable garden peers towards the railway line and Kennet and Avon canal.

"Up between Burbage Wharf and New Mill the canal and railway run side by side. It is a horrible place to ride because the towpath has canal on one side and railtrack on the other. The Torbay express, which had a steam-engine in those days, came speeding down making a horrific swish-swish noise. It was a terrible place for horses. I rode many miles up and down that towpath going from Stanton to Pewsey and Wootton Rivers, and it was always tricky.

"There are two bridges you cannot go under, the iron bridge before Pewsey, and the Wharf bridge. They were the worst. Other bridges you rode under and father's horses were trained to do them. The authorities have tried to stop people riding the towpath ever since 1966. And I have invited them to prosecute me! But they are afraid to do so, as I have ridden it man and boy for sixty years." However, his face showed he did not look too cheerful about it!

He went to fetch a tape he had recorded, so it came to mind that there is a story that Monty was once asked how deep the canal was.

"I used to cross it regularly. Not deep at all," Monty said with a completely straight face. And Peter Horton and Morris Nicol took his word for it and went in near Cocklebury Farm, with water so deep it closed right over their horses' heads.

"Never been in it in my life," chuckled Monty. "Never been in." He was able to say the most outrageous things to his friends without causing any offence.

Jim continued with his story.

"Fred Howes, who was a great character, lived by the canal and farmed at Inlands Farm, opposite Stowell crossroads. Lord Melchett used to give him horses when they got too old for Hunt service. Do anything for Lord Melchett would Fred, and always had a fox for Boxing Day. He was a large man, and rode out with a big stick stuck in his gumboot. A real character.

"The railway line outside Andover was a problem, because in those days from a meet at Redenham, when Philip Dunn was field Master, the fox came straight out of Redenham Park and across the railway with hounds close behind him. There was a fast train every three-quarters of an hour and the only way across was through two kissing gates one each side. To go through you had to have a sensible sort of horse, and back him into the gate, then push. Cross the railtrack and do the same thing in reverse.

"One of the whips crossed by the bridge lower down, and away we went with hounds to Little Shoddesden, then Kimpton and up to Ashdown Copse, where the fox went to earth above the cricket ground at Tidworth. As nobody seemed to appear we collected hounds and started off back. Meantime the huntsman had ridden forwards into the kissing gate, but he couldn't get him to back out. The worst thing happened! A train came along and frightened the horse to death, and it took him half an hour to extricate himself. Philip was none too pleased that we had left them all behind."

Two watercolours of local summer scenes hanging above the dining-table were painted by the Vicar of Overton. A study of the dry, sandy road leading from Adam's Grave, down through cool, green trees to Alton Turnpike looks towards Woodborough where the road crosses the railway line. The picture speaks of building and repairing hunt jumps in hot sunshine.

"Another man who was of great strength to the Tedworth was Morris Nicol. He used to hunt on foot as a boy with Fred Howe's son Joe. Demobbed from the Air Force after the war, he got some terriers and for many years was a wonderful terrierman and did a lot of good.

"His father was a gypsy and he started G. B. Nicol at London House, Pewsey. They said he sold ribbon by the foot, and had a shoe shop and a wool shop. Also they used to do second-hand furniture and tents. He lent marquees to father, and took chairs to Tedworth House for the hunt ball. We all ate chicken supplied by Morris Nicol. And he used to help with jumps. I'd take a man and he'd take a man and we'd go all through Wootton Rivers and up to New Mill. Then he bought a horse and started hunting. But that was after he's finished with the terrier work.

"Another interesting character was Lady Rosemary Brudenell-Bruce. She whipped-in during the time of George Goodwin and later Len Lloyd. One day Goodwin and his first whipper-in both fell off and broke their legs hunting the Ranges on Salisbury Plain. Lady Rosemary, Morris Nicol and Jack Kunkler* collected hounds to take them back to Sunnyhill. For six long weeks Lady Rosemary hunted the pack with Jack turning hounds to her, and every day she drove to kennels to help with flesh, and feed the hounds. She did a wonderful job.

"Later on she started the Savernake Forest Buckhounds, with Elizabeth Young as Secretary and her whipper-in, although the only buck killed was on the London road by a lorry. The speed and danger of the A4 traffic made hunting treacherous. Unfortunately, hounds rioted into the deerpark and Lord Cardigan, Lady Rosemary's brother, shot three of them. He threatened to shoot her if they went in again! Finally she gave up, and went in for bloodhounds. But", said Jim, "although we had a bit of fun it was a little too slow." And his face softened.

The Hunt Committee had accepted Mr. J. M. Read's offer to take over the mastership from 1 May 1965, after the resignation of the three joint Masters.

"I have spent a lot of my own money at kennels," Mr. Dalgety appears to have said to Brigadier Walch. "I have been here a year and now you kick me out!" It had been a bad year with poor weather and a shortage of foxes.

Jim commented, "But Dalgety wasn't the least bit difficult. Charming . . .

**Jack Kunkler was the landlord of the Greyhound Hotel in Pewsey as was his father before him, and it was the great hunting hotel for meetings after the war.*

Tedworth meet at Rainscombe Park.
L to R: Alison Read (now Mrs. Jones), Bryan Read Esq., Monty Read Esq., Jim Read Esq., Tony Herring and Ted Burton.

. . perfect gentleman about the whole thing. Perhaps he realised it had been a mistake. At a meet at Overton he said that he would be pleased to help me, before or after the change. Strange man. I think Mrs. Jonas was a friend! The next ,season Hugh Dalgety came back and hunted a few days with us. It must have taken some doing! They did a lot of work at kennels. Spent a deal of money."

The long hall with its half-panelling of Swedish pine leads to glass doors through which interesting mauve-pink sofas and chairs stand in a very large Nordic lounge. Red poppies and blue cornflower decorate a glass vase on the hall table, the scarlet blooms accentuating red coats in the presentation oil painting displayed above, like an altar piece.

"There are three generations of Reads in the picture. Father, myself, Bryan and little Alison. All of us there." He looks sombre walking down the brick path. Across the drive are modern timber loose-boxes in his small yard.

"In my day the farmers hunted. They all came out. You had a horse to ride round the farm in the morning, and another for hunting. Now it's all those four-wheel drives. No farmers out these days." And his face was inexorably sad.

Soon after taking up the reins, the new Master was invited by the Duke of Beaufort to hunt the Yatesbury, Winterbourne Bassett and Broad Hinton country which lies over the hill and to the west of Marlborough Downs. Formerly the Craven hunted this parcel of land, but there had been disagreement. The arrangement with the Tedworth continued happily for several years and was a valuable extension for us, until farmers began to complain.

"You only come," they said, "when you cannot hunt your own side."

Major Gundrey, joint Master of the Beaufort, felt it hard on farmers that two packs should hunt over the ground, especially as a great deal of Tedworth country was under-hunted due to the absence of foxes. There was a greater need than ever before for co-operation between hunting and shooting people and to ensure that coverts were properly foxed with more litters kept in the country generally. Otherwise how could any hunt survive?

Len Lloyd was getting old and crotchety, a fate that must come to all of us. Also he was difficult to work with. Nobody stayed long. After many years of service it was agreed that a young amateur Master be approached to carry the horn.

Even as a small boy William Nunneley sought every opportunity to visit kennels near his home, and in this way was connected with the Hursley and V.W.H. hunts. An enchanting fellow, he was young and ambitious being very keen to prove himself. His photograph in the local paper at the Hunt Supporters' supper in the Foresters Hall, Pewsey, shows an eager, pleasant twenty-year-old holding a glass of whisky. The four men in the picture smile broadly. Next to William is Group Captain Stansfeld, his head framed by a dartboard, looking like a bucolic halo. Len Lloyd, a good head shorter than William, shows a grin to proclaim that twenty-five years of hunting have knocked front-teeth out, while P. D. Deacon and Gordon Cleall, who was Jim Read's foreman at Kennet, are obviously having a happy evening.

Incidentally William was renowned for his love of the good time, girl friends and song!

He lived at kennels in the second half of the cottage. Drains were a problem and extensive repairs, including inside decorations, cost £600 making a continual call on finances. With his infectious enthusiasm William learned to be a very good huntsman, and stayed with us only two seasons, when he left the Tedworth for the Morpeth.

April 30th, 1970, was Len Lloyd's last day as kennelman. He was presented with a silver hunting-horn and a cheque for £500. Major Charles Ashton said that Len's work was not confined to the hunting field. There was much work to be done at kennels, and he always succeeded in keeping hounds in a fine condition.

The following season shows Tony Herring, from the Albrighton Woodland in Warwickshire, as kennelhuntsman, with Ted Burton taking first whipper-in and Mr. Bryan Read as amateur second whip.

A great deal of interest was being shown in the Pony Club, under the vigorous direction of Mr. Barry Wookey as District Commissioner for over ten years. Major General G. W. E. Heath was the first D.C., when a very strange character took the Pony Club helm. They say he was so poor that he cut up the roofing timbers of a manorhouse where he lived to keep his fire alight!

Barry Wookey was a first class D.C., and being a great perfectionist he brought the children up to a very high standard. The team qualified for the Pony Club Championships in the One Day Event, but were eliminated at Stoneleigh. He felt it better for children to try to do whatever was on tap at the moment rather than have an elite on very expensive ponies trained by mum.

At the Pony Trials over a hundred outside people helped with tents, food and competitions, while at camp the children even had an orchestra. The music may not have sounded too good to a musician, but everyone was very proud of them.

In 1972 Mrs. Mary Robinson became D.C. Her husband, Lieutenant Colonel Robinson, was a keen supporter and member of the Hunt Committee, and they lived in a pink Georgian house at Beechingstoke. As well as being talented with the children as an instructress, Mrs. Robinson would sit for hours near the window to give her daylight for the exquisite embroidery work which made her locally famous. Railway trains which appear to have such a special affinity for hunting in Pewsey Vale rattle past the garden, while horses in stables pull contentedly at hay nets.

Mrs. Penny Portman was District Commissioner to take over with one hundred and fifty children, and she and Chris Morgan-Smith remember camp for juniors at Stowell Park. Lady Rothschild is marvellously kind, and allowed them to camp between the house and stables. But they must beware of George Stollery the gardener! And had to be frightfully careful to leave no marks on the grass. During the day, children did their ponies and enjoyed games, also jumping competitions.

Comments from one holding the honourable position as President of the branch says it can be seen all happening again.

"The workers who can always be relied upon to do the dirty jobs. The flash ones who want to instruct and know it all. The knowledgeable ones who really do know it all but are backward in coming forward, and the plain nuisances! I trust you will not quote me on this! I shall deny everything! But the children are the same — below thirteen they are a pleasure to teach, above that age they become blasé until they reach about eighteen when they become useful again. In short, nothing changes, only as we get older we are able to stand back and enjoy the unfolding scene!"

The children were allowed to use the games room, with shrieks of joy squealing over the box-hedges which make windbreaks for the swimming-pool. After tea, disruptive ponies were led to stabling, while the well-mannered darlings were turned out in the park. Good cover lies to the east, with a belt of trees planted to shelter pasture and the triangle of country lanes.

At dusk, looking across the grass to this pale, enclosed house of hunting recollections, white summer haze embroiled smoke from camp fires to hold close the comforting smell of barbecued sausages and burgers. Childish voices in the apple time of summer holidays might have piped:

"There were ten green bottles hanging on a wall . . . . ."

For the past few years the senior camp has been held at Standen Manor, the home of the present D.C. Mrs. Susie McGrath. She tells us that up to sixty children at a time sleep in horseboxes or trailers with ponies either stabled or turned out. Many amusing incidents have happened over the years. One pony knew it all as he had been at camp for many years with different owners.

"Ha-ha," he said evading a squad of pink-cheeked little riders, desperate to catch him before breakfast. Fed up and terrified of missing their bacon and eggs the children walked back to stables. The pony then calmly jumped the fence, trotted back to stables and was last seen enjoying his breakfast, before the children turned kitchenwards for theirs.

The Tedworth Hunt Supporters' Club was started at Leigh Hill on 14 October 1964 with Group Captain Stansfeld as the first chairman. Its main object is to bring out and encourage the goodwill of the countryside towards hunting. Originally the Club was not envisaged as being of financial assistance to the Hunt. With a subscription of 2/6d (12½p) membership rose to three hundred.

Skittles matches between mounted and unmounted members seem to have been the first event, with the annual working-terrier show as the centre-piece of activities, subsequently there were film evenings showing footage from the Savernake Forest Buckhounds, Courtenay Tracy Otterhounds as well as the Tedworth Hunt, shot by Brigadier Walch. And the perennial moonlight steeplechases with barn dances run alternately by the Hunt or T.H.S.C. They seemed to vie with each other for evocative dance bands, such as *King's Korner*, the *Original Shades* and *Shag Connors and the Carrot Crunchers*. On a wind-swept hilltop on Major Ashton's land at the head of Milton Combe, the gamekeepers of Pewsey Vale met the T.H.S.C. in a clay-pigeon shoot. But even the youth and enthusiasm of William Nunneley could not save the T.H.S.C. from being vanquished 143 to 104 points. However, the refreshments at Pewsey were excellent.

A bicycle point-to-point was combined with the terrier show at Manton Grange, by kind permission of Roger Roberts and Mr. and Mrs. Scrimgeour, while the 200 Club was born during John Jones' long chairmanship. (See Appendix.)

During a lawn meet at Church Farm, Stanton, in 1975, Sir William Beale, joint Master 1972-81, accepted the keys of a Ford Transit 115 van, purchased with money raised by the Club. And a seasonal Christmas gift of a lorry capable of transporting three horses and the hounds, costing £1400, underlined the Club's commitment to financial assistance. Gifts of electrical drainage pumps, endless repairs to kennels, and the purchase of horses, have continued over the years from fund-raising cheese and wine parties, barbecues, quizzes, inter-hunt show-jumping competitions with the R.A., Vine and Craven, Old Berks and Avon Vale, and a host of other attractive events.

Today it is doubtful if any hunt can survive without the strong support of a loyal and dedicated Hunt Supporters' Club.

But perhaps the most crucial factor in the annals of the Hunt has been the support given by large influential farmers, notably the Wookeys, Reads, Hortons and Swantons. Frank Swanton was originally manager for the Meux Estates of Lockeridge, Overton and West Woods. He then bought his own farm at West Overton expanding to 2500 acres. Later he gave each of his three sons a farm. Gilly has now retired and moved to East Grafton, while Roger and his Irish wife, with her horse and two ponies for the children, farms East Kennet-West Overton land. Robin specialises in disease-free pigs to the north of the A4 road. Without the support of farmers all hunting dies!

In years, there may be only four or five hunts that are truly memorable. On such a day, the field unboxed at Westcourt and followed hounds across the fields to Bowden's Farm. This was regarded as our best triangle of country. Mr. Tom Curnick greeted hounds with port and cake, before the pack was taken to draw his kale. A strong fox was soon afoot.

The Master could scarcely get the field going before his mare showed signs of being tucked up with azoturia, so he shouted for his second horse. He is inclined to be philosophical about such calamities even though he is not known to smile. Hounds, fifty yards behind their pilot, drove on towards Ram Alley. To the Master's chagrin, the second horse was tacked up with a point-to-point saddle. There was no time to change, and the field was led over Wharf Bridge to Leigh Hill copse. A moment's check, then off again up the hill skirting the disused railway to Brick Hill Copse, and so on towards Clench Common.

Before gaining the bottom end of Withycopse, the hunt had to ride gaps in the entrenchment made by small, nimble, horned sheep, the ancestors of Wiltshire Horn flocks. Still galloping stripes of green turf marking open downland tracks across sky-touching crests, the cry grew fainter. After the fastest hunt of the season, hounds were disappointed when the fox suddenly disappeared in Boreham Woods.

Difficulties with the country shared with the R.A. had been nagging for years. At a meeting on 24 July 1964 chaired by Lieutenant General Sir Kenneth Darling, and attended by Colonel Kidston-Montgomerie, A. W. H. Dalgety, M. J. Read, Brigadier Walch, together with Lieutenant Colonel F. B. "Freddy" Edmeades, and T. Davidson, the R.A. secretary, a complicated arrangement had sectioned the country into brown, blue and yellow, also red and green areas. Agreement was made for a number of days hunting per month to be given to the R.A. In practice, the two huntsmen organised hunting in an informal friendly fashion.

By 1971 there was a profusion of taut letters and meetings. It was thought that the R.A. were becoming charming poachers! And taking too many foxes! This was exacerbated by understandably hurt feelings amongst some elder Tedworth members who found it difficult to accept that times had changed. Modern warfare had come to stay, and War Office artillery and rifle ranges were occupying traditional tribal hunting grounds.

In 1972 the blue country, roughly Bulford Ranges, was still in contention. The Tedworth wrote to say they intended to reserve hunting to themselves, with the exception of some form of combined meet, where caps at Tedworth rates would be payable to them.

At a very difficult meeting in a house near Savernake, and chaired by Brigadier E. G. B. "Gris" Davies Scourfield, with the new R.A. Master Lieutenant Colonel Peter Heaton-Ellis, it was pointed out that we hunting people must stick together. The country in question is Army land. In military terms it is not Tedworth country though it may be in the eyes of the Masters of Foxhounds' Association. But if the R.A. cannot hunt then the Tedworth cannot hunt either. Although the R.A. did not want to force the issue, the argument that the Army commander must decide as landlord, how often and by whom his land should be hunted appeared to carry weight. The matter was argued fiercely by both sides and nearly got out of hand, but eventually tact and compromise won the day. After a season of suspicion, excellent relations with the Tedworth were restored.

That season Mr. Jim Read resigned the mastership as he felt there was not sufficient country support to give two good days' hunting a week with the requisite number of foxes. He loves fishing. Solitary and patient he casts a dryfly on the cool, deep water of the Bowood Reservoir at Calston, where large trout move at ease in their universe. Steep, high banks thick with trees, shelter this hidden, secret valley where ice-green water pours over the weir. It is a favoured place - a combe like a drowned angel.

During the 'seventies Monty continued to go out hunting. Although he did not jump, he was never without his spurs and, of course, always wore his famous mackintosh. Perhaps he felt cold. The raincoat exists, and is worn occasionally by the family for comfort and protection.

Hunting with the Beaufort, horses travelled in a hired lorry, and the man was given ten shillings to wait all day, as Monty never learnt to drive a horsebox. A picture of him with Lady Moyne and Peter Horton shows his steady, fifteen-hand horse, with its hogged mane, wearing a muzzle! Because as he said:

"He will eat grass! Pulls my arms out!"

At eighty-seven, like so many aged sportsmen, he seemed to have a

MAP NUMBER 2

Scale approx. 1: 200.000

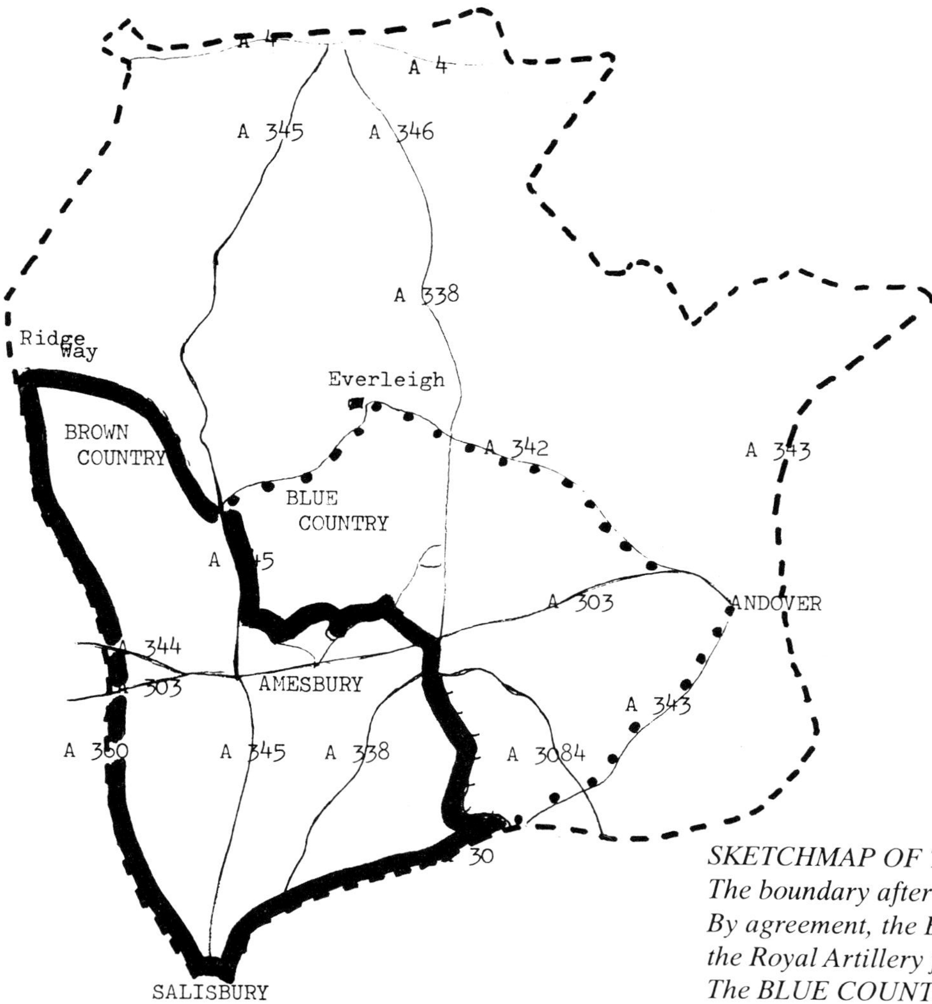

SKETCHMAP OF TEDWORTH HUNT COUNTRY
The boundary after W.W.2 is virtually the same as Map 1 — — — —
By agreement, the BROWN COUNTRY is now on permanent loan to the Royal Artillery foxhounds.
The BLUE COUNTRY is hunted by both the Tedworth and the R.A.H.

premonition of death. One Sunday lunch-time he said he hoped to die of a heart attack.

The autumn morning was bright and sunny. It was Thursday 16 October and Monty rode the old horse quietly to the top of Milk Hill.

"It's the best morning I've had," he told the tractor driver. "The very best," and he turned down the chalk trackway towards Stanton. But he never got home.

Walking past the favourite Dogrun field, maybe his beloved greyhounds appeared to race for the last time from the barn and past the willow stands to Dogrun Covert, their vision hanging on the aether of the field.

Meantime, Rhonda Small and Stuart Legg were on exercise along the trackway running north from All Cannings towards Tan hill, when they saw him on the lower road, halfway between the meeting of the tracks and the barn.

Monty waved to them. Then he just tumbled off his horse. The gelding just stood there. He never moved as Rhonda and Stuart galloped down their track and back again towards him. He was quite dead.

Perhaps Jim had the penultimate word:

"The old man died with his spurs on."

"But," said a lady after the church service, where the press was so great that an overflow had to be accommodated in the Church Hall,

"It's not so much a question of his spurs being on, as how did he manage to put them on at his age? I have to get my husband to help me."

Chapter 12

The Halcyon Days

Biddeston House.

The 1972 season opened with the advent of four new Masters, Lady Moyne, Sir William Beale, Captain Charles Spencer and Mr. Peter Horton, who hunted hounds as an amateur. Tony Herring had left the Hunt's service, so Ted Burton became kennelhuntsman. Mr. Bryan Read and the Honourable Kieran Guinness were amateur whippers-in.

Peter Horton rode first when he was only three, at his home in Cricklade. Aged twelve, he exercised his father's racehorses and was taking them to assorted point-to-point meetings. In 1952, he came to Tedworth country to farm at Puckshipton, where he became known as a bold rider across those wire-infested fields, so few could follow him. Peter also served on the Hunt Committee, and in 1970 was secretary of the point-to-point committee.

Moving to Widdington Farm, Upavon, in 1971 he and his wife Bunty built up an excellent string of hunters and point-to-pointers. However, never having hunted hounds, it was a difficult challenge to take on the pack and show sport.

It takes several seasons for a new huntsman to learn the type of hound that suits his country. Therefore, he sought the vast experience of the late Duke of Beaufort, and with the help of majestic Beaufort records the original Tedworth bloodlines were traced back. Like Sir Peter Farquhar he suspected that a light, racy foxhound should be bred for hunting trackways. As early as 1973 the F.K.S.B. shows the Duke of Beaufort's Bluecap '71 and V.W.H. Planter '70 used as stallion hounds.

During a meeting at the Greyhound Hotel, Pewsey, his field Master Sir William Beale said that they had already killed more foxes during cub-hunting than for many years past. Peter was indeed lucky that for twelve years he was to have a splendid Secretary in Major J. F. L. Clarke. Always tactful, he possessed the delightful manner of smiling through the tribulations and pitfalls which lurk during any secretaryship.

At the opening meet in Rainscombe Park, hounds sat in a tight group with every eye on the Master. They quivered with anticipation, whining softly. Hunting hounds is a matter of enthusiasm, and Peter Horton is a very special person, with the Tedworth lucky to have had him.

"It's his enthusiasm that counts," says Peter. "Hounds must respect you. The huntsman must want the job, otherwise hounds won't respect him. If he is enthusiastic, then hounds catch the excitement. Anticipate a good day, and do everything the huntsman wants. They know!"

Speaking of Sir William as field Master, Peter explained:

"Billy Beale was very good and always gave me a bit of room. Coming from the Grafton he had fox sense and listened to the wind. He was of the old school and believed you don't jump unless hounds are running. He was very strict and allowed no skylarking, with no galloping about, which is boring for the field if things are slow. Lady Moyne used to go off, and make her own way. She is always very sweet, fey almost, and never got bawled out!"

When Billy first came it was inevitable that he was nicknamed "the Grocer". Sir William Francis Beale O.B.E. was born in 1908 and educated at Downside and Pembroke College, Cambridge. He was Chairman of Green's Stores (Ilford) the multiple grocers, Chairman of the N.A.A.F.I. and also a Director of the British West African Corporation Ltd. Knighted in 1956 he married Hynek Zaloudek, known as Baie. A kind man, Billy always wanted to know how you were and what you were doing. He attended race meetings with Judy Grange, England's sole lady starter.

Before moving to The Grange, All Cannings, his Rolls Royce parked outside white, thatched China Cottage near Stowell Park, showed that Sir William and Lady Beale were at home. Sir Philip Dunn was non-plussed.

"How," he is reputed to have said, "how can a chap living in a cottage afford a Rolls Royce, when I have had to sell my Bentley?" But then Sir Philip was always pleading poverty! Having inherited several million from his father's estate, and being an intelligent, well-organised man himself, his parsimony was a mere whim.

"Morning Master!" is the caption given to Stanley Hurwitz's report and photographs of the meet at Stowell Drier on 21 September 1974. Billy, riding a heavy horse, blanket clipped and with large feet, is saluting Jeremy Robb, while Peter leads an attentive pack to draw Stowell Park, where Sir Philip always had a fox for hounds. Morris Nicol is pictured leaning on his horse's neck to listen with a terrierman's acute awareness, his bowler hat angled on the back of his head, perhaps to act like an amplifying dish.

A cub breaks cover from an earth and hounds are away for a short burst before losing him in Park Copse. The early sun is becoming warmer and the pack is led across stubble, past Huish and towards the cool of Gopher Wood. Peter belongs to the silent school of huntsmen allowing hounds to work with minimum interference.

Horses scramble up the steep path of the Earthworks, pushing their way through thorn and bramble. The scent of over ripe cherryplum and Michaelmas russets fill the air. Children have blackberry mouths and rosebrier scratched faces.

The pace is leisurely. It is too hot. Gopher Wood proves blank, until a holloa tells the huntsman that the cub is afoot again. Mr. Hurwitz's last photograph shows when Peter signals that the cub has gone to ground.

Nineteen seventy-six brought great sadness to Stowell Park, when Sir Philip Dunn died at the age of seventy. His obituary underlines that he was a many-sided character. A shy man, it was not easy for any one person to fathom all his qualities. Totally without vulgarity, he had an excellent eye for paintings and furniture. He married Lady Mary Sybil St. Clair-Erskine, but was divorced. In 1969 they remarried, but it was said that they could not live together, and they could not live apart.

Peter rented Widdington Farm from the War Department, and the house shelters in the deeply-etched, upthrusting hillside which descends two hundred feet to the Avon river, to form the eastern flank of the Plain. Casterley Camp crowns the Earthworks, to guard the south and western legs of the Ridgeway. Here bordering the road, hundreds of sheep nibble grass, blue with dog violets, also wild thyme, rockroses and eyebright. Thirteen different kinds of orchids may be found on the Impact Area.

Peter felt that as he farmed at Widdington, he should hunt there. So, he and Barry Wookey, of Upavon Manor, joined forces. Fortunately, Lieutenant Colonel Heaton-Ellis is always friendly and co-operative. It was agreed that only the Tedworth hunted the northern corridor to include Rushall Hill, Charlton Clump and Marden Cowbag which leads to the Honeystreet, Church Farm and Woodborough sections.

The 1977-78 season started late. A dry summer followed by a great deal of rain meant corn being harvested late. At Widdington scent was excellent although not too many cubs were about. Perhaps they still enjoyed foraging the corn. Two goodish hunts with lots of jumping ended with an old fox marked to ground in the garden. David Jones, the new terrierman, came out, with Ted Burton on Henry, a great wire jumper. A talented horseman, Ted just taps the wire to give it movement and then jumps.

Military planning is a laborious affair! Everything must be authorised and approved in advance. Therefore, both R.A. and Tedworth Masters had to organise their meets twelve months ahead. Shooting interests at Bulford had also to be circumnavigated, and needed a great deal of tact. It was fortunate that a pleasant and relaxed atmosphere existed between the two huntsmen. Only a few caustic remarks lingered on amongst committees.

A cracking good day was from Fosbury on 16 February, and horses unboxed at Maurice Bryant's Farm. He is a staunch friend to the Tedworth. Lady Moyne wearing her green velvet cap, with a flower in her buttonhole to show mastership, rode Daniel, a lovely chestnut Anglo-Arab bred by her at Biddesden. She always wore the first flower of spring. Perhaps it was witch-hazel, the first primrose and always the first violet. Lady Moyne became Master with great encouragement from Jim Read. Light morning mist swathed steep little valleys and extensive woods. She and Pam Antrobus rode on past small pasture and shaggy, old stubble of the famous three-thousand acre shoot belonging to Kit Garnett who was Bill Govett's step-father. At the meet Peter was riding one-eyed Nelson, and his field Master was Captain Charles Spencer out with his wife Cherry.

Fred Oxford, then head keeper, showed us plenty of foxes and hounds found quickly. Although scent was poor in the morning, the pack persevered to hunt along good trackways into Craven country.

Four Tedworth Masters.
L to R: C. G. C. Spencer, Lady Moyne, Peter Horton, Monty Read.

Later in the day they drew Thorneycombe, and what a terrible place it is for flints! Captain Spencer said that we need two rails here. Hounds found in Oakhill Wood and they simply screamed off. Hounds raced right round the wood, as though they were going to Cherringtons. The field hesitated one minute. And the pack was gone! One-eyed Nelson was a barbed wire expert, and the huntsman jumped the wire fence which protects warm covert where pheasants strut.

They heard them far away. Hounds were sometimes half a mile ahead of the huntsman, running over bracken and heath, with jays shrieking when put up, and flocks of wood-pigeons agitated at the turmoil.

For two hours at racing pace they ran the Test Way to Linkenholt. Then bypassing Sheepless Hill hounds mounted eleven hundred foot Inkpen where they gave a stout fox best.

With darkness falling Peter gathered up his hounds. Making his way back towards the meet, he waved down a car.

"The way to Fosbury?" he asked.

"Never heard of it," came the reply. And the local closed his window to shut out an icy February night.

Meanwhile finding themselves left behind, had subscribers who lived near Ludgershall decided to go home early, they would have hacked past Conholt House. Memories linger here. The Duke of Wellington, while out with the Tedworth, used this beautiful demesne as a hunting-box. Following Chute Causeway, our riders would then turn south, where the spire of Chuteforest Church brings more tumbled memories. Nearby at Chute Lodge Mr. Osmond, the butcher of Vernham, delivered meat to the Reverend Henry Fowle's kitchen, before donning his black coat to join the hunt at

Longbotton Farm. Woolly sheep, ring coverts and partridges are the same although extensive woodland has its crop of conifers, and maize rattles in some small fields.

In the valley Biddesden House stands at the crossroads. This is the elegant Queen Anne style home of the late Lord Moyne who died in 1992, and Elisabeth, his second wife. Lord Moyne was vice-chairman of Arthur Guinness & Co, famous for their invigorating stout, although his main interests were artistic, charitable and agricultural. He published many books, several for children.

A lovely old gentleman, latterly he is remembered cub-hunting wearing his favourite Irish tweed. At Biddesden meets, Guinness was served as Lord Moyne did not approve of hard spirits, and Barry Wookey is the only person to have succeeded in finding whisky! Of gentle charm and rather quiet nobody seemed to ever defy his wishes. Married first to Diana Mitford, the daughter of Lord Redesdale, they had two sons. By his second marriage to Elisabeth, née Nelson, there are four sons (the eldest dying in 1977) and five daughters. Of vague manner, it is said that Lord Moyne some years ago met Lady Mosley, his first wife, at a party.

"You must be one of the Mitford girls," he said.

The *Arab Horse Society News* tells us: "Lord and Lady Moyne founded the Biddesden Stud in 1939 with the purchase of Starilla and Dafinetta from Lady Wentworth. The stud has flourished and in recent years has been managed by their son the Honourable Finn Guiness. Many fine horses have been produced there and have won success in the showring, in performance events and on the racetrack." And, of course, on the hunting field.

All the family have been seen out hunting over the years and now there is a new generation joining the hunt. Both Erskine and Mirabel have been joint Masters while Finn is vice-Chairman of the Committee. He is a keen conservationist and comes out regularly. Throughout Lady Moyne's mastership her daughter Catriona hunted alongside her mother, mounted on a chestnut Anglo-arab named Radadash, brother to Daniel. Catriona knew the names of hounds, and Peter Horton used to tell her to go to the 'usual place', and she would always know! While at Crossbelts there is 'Catriona's Corner' where she always stood.

Diarmid hunted a great deal before he died, and played polo often on Biddesden Arabs, while his brother Kieran was Master of the Westmeath in Ireland 1973-76 and 1981-85. He is very keen on hounds, and has judged the Tedworth. He also breeds quality Irish hunters. His sister Tamsy used to hunt regularly, while Rosaleen's Indian husband often hunts on his Arab horse.

Returning to our Fosbury epic, Captain and Mrs. Spencer waited for their errant huntsman, and then drove home to Stokke Cottages, Great Bedwyn, where three days later the Hunt enjoyed six bottles of port at their lawn meet.

The gaggle of brave, thatched cottages is a secret world of mottled pasture and trees on Stokke Common. They have been sold or rented by Savernake estate. Set in hedged gardens the tranquillity of the place stills longings for peace and a desire for beauty.

The first draw was the new copse behind Bloxham Lodge*, and Spencer sent Cherry and two others on point, taking the field round to the far side of the covert. Ten minutes of silence. Then a woodcock came out and hounds spoke to a little vixen. But she was not waiting around. She made out towards Stokke and Bedwyn Common, with the field making a good pace across the Common and down the Fir Walk crossing by the Chestnuts. Lady Moyne's Daniel galloped as fast as a train, having the speed of the thoroughbred and agility of the Arab. The fox swung left into the rhododendrons. Being viewed by the huntsman on the road, he gave a later regretted holloa, and made the hounds lift their heads. Here a fresh fox got up.

Jumping a small rail, one of the field had a fall from a new 'chaser he had bought. The loose horse cleared a forest gate beautifully, to evade lots of little girls, pony tails flying and Club ties awry, who were attempting to catch him. Finally he was cornered in a field and Cherry kindly took him away, consequently missing the rest of the hunt.

Charles squeezed through a gap leading to the track down Horsehall Hill. Hounds were speaking in Cobham Firth but were soon back making for Timbridge. His diary, an orange and blue exercise book says:

"We found a nice gate — we being Peter Horton, Elisabeth Moyne and her daughter Catriona. A good upstanding obstacle and still intact. Crossed the road and into the covert again — out over a low rail amongst the bushes which Nellie made little pretence of jumping. I must replace it tomorrow."

That day the hunt petered out, and being short of horses, the huntsman took hounds home.

Charles was in charge of the wire fund from 1966-72 which is essential for keeping a country open. Each hunting report in his diary is headed with notes such as:

"Rails 1. Opposite Bedwyn Common.
2. London ride, two, over Stokkes grass.
3. Cobham Firth. North of Timbridge — others."

Volunteers put up the fences themselves, carrying poles across the fields and driving in posts. On his becoming Master, Cherry took over the task 1972-93. The July 1981 minutes report that seventy-four jumps were repaired or built, and eight gates supplied and placed in position at a cost of £1250 in labour and £458 in materials.

In January 1978 Charles resigned as joint Master due to increased business commitments.

"How is this for comfort?"

is the title of an hilarious photograph taken by Stanley Hurwitz of Captain Spencer and Jim Read sitting on a stone garden seat presented to Charles as a gift by grateful Hunt supporters. The seat still stands in Stokke Cottage garden. Stables are empty of horses now. But trees of Savernake Forest Outliers lap the back of the lawn in a green, deep sea, leaving it like a bucolic, pastoral island in an England that he feels has purpose but no peace.

Three years later Sir William Beale relinquished his mastership. At

**Extracts from his diary by kind permission of Captain Charles Spencer.*

seventy-three he considered a younger man should take his place. Lady Moyne resigned at the same time, and hung up her green hat until her daughter Mirabel could wear it as Master. Meantime winter flowers watched in Biddesden gardens when Erskine Guinness, young-looking, blonde and a natural horseman continued the family tradition as Master for three seasons. Hunting being in his Irish blood, he is a really good field Master. A keen farmer, he studied agriculture at Edinburgh, and became a Wiltshire County Councillor. Erskine lived at Crawlboys Farm and now resides at Fosbury Manor. The Biddesden estate includes Crawlboys and Mount Orleans with arable, sheep and cattle all farmed together, Mount Orleans being Erskine's special interest. Bryan Read also joined Peter as Master. Colin Cooper, noted for a black beard and red armband, became a fourth joint for one season only, when business difficulties forced him to move away.

Snow prevented hunting for two weeks when 16 January 1982 hounds met at Crawlboys Farm. Guinness hospitality was hot, to warm icy fingers and toes. Hounds were hunted on foot by Peter with Erskine as field Master. A fox was soon disturbed in Collingbourne with the pack fastening on to the line, which took them through Heron's, Great Stonehedge and Great Wickheath Copses.* Here scent failed, as did aching legs unused to snow-running. Most of the field repaired to cars and scalding drinks, only the huntsman drove on for over two hours. The hounds enjoyed themselves hugely.

Of all events in the spring calendar the hunt point-to-point is the most eagerly awaited, as well as being of great financial importance. Held at Larkhill for thirty years when racing moved to Barbury Castle, Peter Horton was point-to-point secretary until 1972, when Roger Roberts was appointed in his place, to hold the position for fifteen years. This proved a most amicable arrangement.

Roberts was already a member of the point-to-point committee and had suggested a four mile rather than three miles for the Men's Open Race. Viscount Savernake was persuaded to lend an imposing silver gilt cup, to be competed for annually.

Opened in 1947 Larkhill racecourse, with its panoramic views, can be a wild place, unless the sun smiles. Meetings are shared with local hunts and the United Services point-to-point.

Roberts in his book *Forty Years Between the Flags* speaks of the massive amount of paperwork generated:

"1973 was my first meeting as secretary, and as the day drew near I spent so much time on the phone to Horton that the latter must have thought that he might as well have done the job himself. However, in the end the day passed off without mishap with the four mile race being considered another success. The first three home, Rich Rose, Limeburner and All a Myth, being well known performers."

The next year waggons for the use of sponsors, advertisers and the press were produced for the first time. To spectators, Salisbury Plain at her enigmatic loveliest lies beyond the racecourse, with undulating hills and

**Account taken from Peter Flemming's diary who wrote for Horse and Hound as J.E.F.*

valleys like spacetime in constant vibration. Ell barrow, Ell meaning conspicuous, lies to the far north-west with hazy grey sky melding to midnight-blue strip hedges. Rings of beechtrees and nitrogen-rich nettle mark where farms once stood, now extinguished by the War Department. Below, east of Round Covert, was once the polo ground where officers from Netheravon played and hunted with Peter Farquhar.

The press were well looked after! They, together with the Committee and sponsors, enjoyed luncheon, while drinks were served during the entire afternoon. Beyond the green and white striped tents "'Ave it on with Avalon" was heard with shouted odds from bookmaker's lines.

In 1981 the Portmans presented a gold cup as a perpetual trophy for the winner of the four mile race. Known as the *Tedworth Open Race* cup, Penny unearthed it from a broom cupboard in her brother's house in Kingston Warren, her brother being the flat race trainer Henry Candy. The cup was engraved as the *Lutwych Cup* and had been presented by Candy ancestors many years before. After being cleaned it was decided not to re-engrave it but to put the necessary details on the plinth to include the names of Viscount Savernake's gold cup winners, that had been returned.

An ambitious fund-raising event was the ox roast at Tedworth House on 29 June 1985. What would Mr. Assheton Smith have said? The prime organisers were Mr. K. Mendenhall and David and Avril Hammerson. Tickets cost £10 each and ten were sent to each subscriber. There were some loured brows over the question of making up the balance on any tickets unsold. Also the two, eight hundredweight bullocks needed for the roast posed a problem until the Army came to the rescue with a truck and small mobile crane.

On the night, many people nobody had ever seen before converged from every direction, and there were hundreds of cars. Even the military joined in. Disco music hammered out. Gerry Beaton recalls that she stood for hours with the Hammersons at the entrance to one marquee to hand glasses of white wine and welcome guests. Straw bales were provided as seats, which are prickly for summer frocks. In a long tent, chefs resplendent in tall hats served steaks and jacket potatoes carved from the roast.

In spite of the £13,000 taken for tickets expenses were high. However, profits were made to help Hunt finances.

At the 1984 AGM Peter Horton said that the hounds had caught kennel cough which had hit them quite badly, while the next year he reported that cough had affected hounds even more than first thought. This, coupled with two severe periods of frost, had made it a difficult season.

Looking through studbooks, 1973 saw V.W.H. Planter '70 on our own Contact '68, through their progeny Placid, Planet and Plastic, contribute to some of the best hounds in kennels. In 1974 the bitches Wilma '69, Willow '68 and Wistful '68 were used. Their pedigree date back through the "W" line to Winsome '41, and thus to the small nucleus of hounds cared for by Will James during W.W.2.

The good bitch Bluebell '74 was sired by the Duke of Beaufort's Bluecap '71 out of Colour '69, a bitch who with many others represented the Tedworth "C" line dating from days when the pack was recreated in 1949.

Establishment of the "W" line continued from 1977 onwards, with New Forest sires also being used extensively. In 1980 New Forest Barrister '78, a Welsh hound through his tail female back to Plas Machynlleth Miller '63, brought much sought after blood into the pack.

At this period, Jack Clark was Secretary for twelve years, to retire in 1983. However, Cherry Spencer helped him during his last two years. She always had a good rapport with farmers and knew how to talk to them. In 1984 Bill and Di Purves took over with Gill Fuller Shapcott. Gill Fuller Shapcott was the daughter of the great hunting supporter/farmer Jack Osmond, who farmed West Kennet Farm which has been bought by the National Trust. During Peter's final two years Mrs. Cherry Spencer became his joint Master.

Major J. F. L. Clarke, Secretary 1972-83, with Miss Rhonda Small, the present Secretary. (The photograph is NOT as captioned in "Hounds, Hares and Foxes of Larkhill".) Major Clarke is riding Marshall, who led the Charge of the Light Brigade in Tony Richardson's film, while Rhonda rides H for Herbert.

The last opening meet was at East Kennet Manor, and Indian summer sun accentuated scarlet coats against the green doors of Dr. Cameron's stable yard. Behind a low brick wall hounds sat lethargic because it was too hot, and scent would be uninteresting. Welcome drinks and ginger cake was carried across lawns from the late Georgian house with its five bays, to seventy mounted followers. It was a happy meet although people coffee-housed and wondered. Peter was leaving, so they say! A hard man to follow. Names for a new Master were being tossed about. Perhaps Dr. Cameron their host?

The huntsman led hounds round the high brick wall of the garden to the withy beds on Kennet river, then to fields of kale. Scent was poor to frustrate his carefully laid hunt plan, which Peter relayed meticulously to his whipper-in. Bryan was field Master that day which he does especially well. Followers took the jumps out of the valley, but made beware of those badger setts on the hill! Galloping the ancient trackways of All Cannings downs, mid-day found hounds and riders on Milk Hill in brilliant sun where far to the south white smoke from the Westbury chimney strode straight up into the sky. The Master blew for home at four o'clock. A disappointing day ended by finding two flat tyres on his vehicle. They took a deal of blowing up!

Today Peter lives at Perry's Farm below Exmoor. He farms two hundred sheep and a herd of beef cattle, although he still rents Widdington land as well. Bunty is in charge of the livery stables, with clients from Essex, London, Hampshire and the U.S.A. to hunt with the Devon and Somerset Staghounds. But they keep in touch with the Tedworth foxhounds.

Chapter 13

Towards the Future

When Peter Horton resigned he left a great void in the Tedworth hunting country.

The two new Masters were Dr. C. B. Cameron M.F.H. 1986-89 and Mr. J. W. Ritchie M.C., M.F.H. 1986-90. Ted Burton was appointed huntsman as neither Master had hunted hounds. David Jones became kennelman with his wife Kathy who helped with the horses. There were three amateur whippers-in, Mr. Bryan Read, Mr. Roger Wheeler and Ted's son Gerald, who is a very keen point-to-point rider.

Mr. James Ritchie lives at Lockeridge Down and had business interests in Africa. He writes that:

"The joint mastership was great fun and entirely harmonious. As far as I can remember we had no quarrels with the Committee, with subscribers or even one another! We were, of course, lucky to have followed Peter Horton who bequeathed us a country where relations between the farmers and the Hunt were excellent."

Dr. Cameron lives at East Kennet Manor, the venue for so many happy meets and interesting hunts from the withybeds and watery meadows of the little Kennet river. At the A.G.M. he said that Ted in his first season had shown keenness and calm. Visiting landowners and farmers is one of the most important aspects of any hunt, and since Ted did most of the picking-up of fallen stock, it was he who kept in friendly touch. And a very good job he made of it! As Peter Horton says:

"He was our ambassador."

With his work in kennels, and hunting hounds twice a week, it was a monumental task for one man!

With greater emphasis on shooting in our hunting country, co-operation with the shoots was of great importance. At Fosbury, one of Ted's best friends was Fred Oxford, headkeeper for seven years on Kit Garnett's 3,000 acre estate, with its high reputation as a private shoot. A greatly respected man, Fred believed that he had his job to do and hunt servants had theirs, so he always kept a fox for us. Also his reputation influenced other keepers not to shoot Charlie to extinction.

Previously Ted had hunted hounds for Peter Horton when he broke his leg and was unable to ride. Roger Wheeler, who has hunted with the Tedworth for thirty years, was whipping-in to him with Richard Whiteway as terrierman. Roger has the Manor Farm Stud at Chisbury, with his four stallions proving themselves in racing under Rules and horse trials. Lord of Arabia is a well-known thoroughbred sire.

Roger remembers Ted's famous instructions:

"Go down there," Ted would say, "go down there and keep your eyes open!"

Although, Roger feels, where "down there" was exactly, seemed to be left to your best imagination. Roger and Bryan Read spent a great deal of time seeing what there was, and where it might be, because Ted, unlike Peter Horton with his meticulous planning, did not always say where he was going! Which made picking-up tail hounds difficult!

"Ted," Roger goes on, "was the best rider over trappy country you have ever seen," so unless you were like Mirabel Helme, the new young Irish lady Master, or her elder brother the Honourable Finn Guinness, at one with your horse, followers often became disillusioned at being left behind to silence and their own chatter. The pack making a habit of disappearing!

During his six seasons as huntsman Ted followed Peter Horton's breeding policy concentrating on sires from the V.W.H. and the Old Berkshire. He used Bardolf, a dark tan dog, to produce a good blue-mottled bitch excellent for hunting tarmac.

By 1989 Dr. Cameron unfortunately became ill and had to give up the mastership, so David Hammerson joined Mirabel. Previously a Master of the South Dorset, 1974-75, with Alistair Jackson, he lives in a rose-coloured Regency house in Everleigh. There are old and new stables for producing yearling thoroughbreds, and breeder-units for thousands of day-old pheasants. David also owns a house in the Lot, France.

His front door stands slightly open. Running feet indicate an enthusiastic welcome. The drawing-room has French furniture with gold legs. There are orchids and an enormous painting dominates one wall.

Mirabel and Erskine speak of the fun of moonlight hunting! And Hammerson writes:

"After a good day at Cross Belts, yet another fox went away, as did hounds, huntsman, Master and field, and the sheer exhilaration of galloping across the Plain caused the adrenalin to flow. Not much jumping ever on the Plain but that night, following Ted on his grey mare, set the blood flowing — shadows appeared to be jumps and the horses loved it. Charlie was given best at The Crown, Everleigh, after one and a half hours in the pitch black at 7.30 p.m."

Changes and more changes came fast afoot. Business interests took James Ritchie away, so that Tim Ormond filled his place as a third Master. A charming man of great integrity, Tim farms in Vine and Craven country at Shepperd's Farm, Draycot Foliat. An attentive and most conscientious field Master nothing, not even "antis", disturbs his equanimity or makes him lose his cool. Listening, he is always listening to hounds. He watches the cattle moving, and observes the birds.

As in Lord Hardwicke's time hounds meet at Sheppard's Farm, combined with Herdwick Farm, during cub-hunting. Drawing a fifty-acre field of maize hounds are interested. Cubs pop out and in again near a line of manhole-covers showing that the Chiseldon Basin, a giant aquifer of spongy, water-bearing rock, must be drained.

A cub darts across the narrow road, and the field take a drop-jump into a meadow to skirt wartime Chisledon Camp. A quick scamper along the old railway line returns through thornbushes to a lane towards the maize. There is a hold-up at a jump.

The field wait politely for the Master, who tackles fences with panache and style. Tim observes as we stand aside:

"I am an old-fashioned Master. Cub-hunting isn't proper hunting. Out hunting, I believe it's every man for himself! If you want to jump . . . good. But if not, there are gates. Nobody is the worse for that!"

Grass is long, lush and sweet. In the west, brown plough climbs the hill above green, colours so green, they accentuate upland tones of peach and blue. The Ridgway leads to the heights of Barbury Castle and the point-to-point course. That morning there is much scampering about between hill, plough and corn, but the chill has evaporated, and there is talk of breakfast!

Tim is particularly popular with farmers, and his knowledge of the country as to where the field can, and cannot go, is vital. He combines an aggressive ability to cross country, with a pleasant manner. Never without a smile, with young people he rarely misses an opportunity to explain what the hounds and huntsman are doing.

Starting in 1988, Di Purves was assisted by Miss Rhonda Small who then took on the very difficult task of Hunt Secretary. Born in Sydney, Australia and formerly a film director, her minutes of meetings are direct and impeccable, with 'bullet' appendices to target important points. A kind hostess, especially towards those persons requiring a bed before cub-hunting and a 4.30 a.m. call, she lives in a cottage, where there are as many crowded bookcases as there are walls to build them on. In the dining/bootroom, Sydney, a beefy black and white cat, lives in a cardboard box. She loves curly, miniature poodles, while in the garden the classical marble bust of a veiled bride, explains that the creative arts and foxhunting are entirely compatible.

She was joined as Secretary by Mr. J. G. C. Jones of Milton Lilbourne, who has hunted with us for twenty-five years. John takes a very special interest in kennels where he does a great deal of work. Children call him Father Christmas because of his scarlet coat, and splendid white beard framing a cherubic face. He is a bellows-maker. A warm-hearted breath to happy hunting!

Two years later Jim Read retired as Chairman. Out hunting, Lucy on her grey pony looks after grandfather, as he follows her with a slow smile. He will not be forgotten.

Mr. John Wallis, who has hunted with the Tedworth since he came down from the Royal Agricultural College, Cirencester, in 1958, was Secretary from 1964 to 1972, and then Treasurer for over seventeen years before becoming Chairman. A land agent and senior partner with Messrs. Humbert, he has farming interests in the Blackmore Vale country. He and Di live at Woodborough at the very heart of the Tedworth country. His father was Air Commodore J. M. B. Wallis of Greystones, County Wicklow. Although John was born in England he still has his Irish roots. By amazing coincidence the next door neighbours at Greystones were a Reverend and Mrs. Jameson, who were the parents of Jim Read's wife, Barbara. With John's parents on active service, he and his sister were brought up by grand-parents in a rambling country house in Lincolnshire. This was real rural life, as Lincolnshire has more great estates than Wiltshire. During the war the children had their ponies, bicycles and lots of animals.

Mr. and Mrs. John Wallis with beloved dogs.
L to R: Daisy, Bright, Poppy and Nell.

Rabbiting with ferrets and terriers was a great sport. John even took his ferret to Stowe; where he could fish in the school lakes. Fishing has always been an interest, and today he takes his rod to a Welsh cottage where he and Di spend their holidays, often at the time of the Royal Welsh Show.

It is his Wiltshire Horn sheep which provide John's chief relaxation and interest. The origin of the breed is unknown, but could date back to Roman times and it is probably a relic of the old Wiltshire Horn which was repeatedly inbred with other breeds. It is one of the largest native breeds of sheep and crossed with a Southdown produce the Oxford Downs. The Wiltshire Horn is unique in having a very short fleece with no wool. Still on the "rare breeds' list" it is, however, no longer an endangered species with well over 2,000 registered breeding ewes in the country. John has won many prizes at the Royal Show, also the Bath and West.

A real country-lover he shoots and likes to work his black labrador bitches. It is due to their country upbringing and country interests that John and Di are able to make such an important contribution to the Tedworth Hunt.

Nineteen-ninety-one was Ted's final season to hunt the pack, although he was to look after hounds and continue as first whipper-in. At Hat Gate, Ted carried the horn for the last time. A photograph presented by the Hunt Supporters' Club shows him riding Ashley, originally bought by Lady Rothschild as an eventer and later sold to the Hunt. He stands in sunshine by a wooded clearing reserved for a Savernake Estates picnic-area.

Bryan Read was now to hunt hounds as Master, the first of his family to do so, although during the 1987-88 season he took the horn when Ted was injured.

With his grey sideburns and smile he knows how to tell a story, and being a Read, tales mean trains! While whipping-in for Peter Horton as he has since 1969, hounds were hunting at the back of Wedhampton. Following a line from the back of Lydeway garage they crossed the railway track just as a train came round the corner. At first it appeared that hounds were hit! But they seemed alright. The train driver applied his brakes being unable to stop for three-quarters of a mile. Bryan galloped after him.

"Sorry. Terribly sorry," he said. "To have let hounds go." The driver was pale, teeth chattering and in a shake all over.

"Alright . . . . . alright . . . . . plenty of room . . . . . plenty." And recovering his breath he pointed with his thumb up the track.

"There's a red-faced Major on the line. On his horse. Thought I might've 'it him. He did not move at all!"

Hound-jogging home that night they puzzled who the red-faced Major might be? Only Colonel Robinson seemed to fit the bill.

A tragic story comes from Patney when Bryan was hunting the pack. A fox was put up and the good hound Savernake led all the way, marking to ground by the railway-line, where an old, iron footbridge crosses near the brick humpback, on the way to All Cannings.

Blowing for home that night the lead two-and-a-half couple hounds did not answer. They had disappeared. Searching the following morning, their bodies were found on the line, although what train it was that killed them and which way it was going was never found out.

Four joint Masters at the Scots Poor meet on 28 January 1992.
L to R: Tim Ormond, Mirabel Helme, David Hammerson and Bryan Read.
(By kind permission of Mr. Trevor Meeks.)

Beautiful and varied as are our traditional meeting places, having contacts in the sporting world David Hammerson thought it would provide much amusement to visit elsewhere. The Cattistock and South Hereford Hunts exchanged meets with us, and Tedworth subscribers had an exciting day negotiating the Mendip Farmers' stone walls.

David has hunted in France for many years and in 1992 took twelve members of the Tedworth, including Ted Burton and Brian Sedgley, to hunt roe deer with L'Equipage de l'Hermite. A long weekend started on the Thursday on a boat to Le Havre, and on the Friday dinner with Baron Bruno de Seroux and his subscribers. Horses were hired for the following day and the Tedworth experienced trotting and La Venerie Francaise. After a good hunt through the forest, a pricket was taken and ceremony took over. Fanfares, wine and a picnic at the end of the day, followed by the Tedworth giving a dinner for sixty for their hosts that night. The lunch, in a small fishing village near Calais on the Sunday, showed that the Tedworth had dispensed with their hangovers and were fit to start again on raw shellfish and wine.

Interesting photographs show elegant blue French hunting dress, and hunting horns which are almost impossible to blow. By his expression, Ted Burton is having the time of his life.

About this time the point-to-point meeting was held at Barbury Castle rather than Larkhill. The Tedworth was the first hunt to open the new course. Alistair Scrimgeour took over as secretary when Roger Roberts retired to Exmoor. Alistair's father, Robin Scrimgeour, is a very prominent figure in the show jumping world as well as being a knowledgeable commentator. His wife, Mrs. Deidre Scrimgeour, is well-known in dressage circles.

Bryan had long wanted to hunt hounds himself, this was his interest when he put in for the mastership. However, with a young family, a poor harvest on the 2,000 acre farm he shares with his brother David, and the administration of a large riding centre, his two seasons proved difficult, and he gave up the horn. At the same time all four Masters resigned.

After much soul-searching with disappointment in some quarters, the conclusion was made that there was no obvious successor to the mastership within the country. Therefore, the Committee agreed to advertise for a Master, fully aware that it was his prerogative to employ his own hunt servant. Of the two potential masters short-listed both wanted to hunt hounds themselves and required to bring their own team. It was therefore with great regret that Ted Burton and David Jones were no longer required, and their testimonial was in excess of £10,000. The final meet for the retiring four Masters was at Upavon on 20 March 1993.

As a very final farewell on 23 March there was a Masters' bye-day. *Countryweek Hunting* reported that the last day of the season will live in the memory! Three packs of hounds — the Tedworth, Cattistock and South Herefordshire - combined to hunt from Mr. and Mrs. Hammerson's meet at Everleigh.

Forty-five and a half couples of hounds were paraded on the lawn before a reputed 150 mounted followers and 350 on foot. The day was fine. Rain from the previous afternoon had left the ground damp, to clear before an early morning frost and cloudless sky. Masters and subscribers from ten packs of hounds were entertained, red and green coats on the lawn imbibed whisky. The paddock drank port and had plenty of food, so that the 'mess bill' must have been prodigious. Then Bryan Read led the combined pack towards Lower Everleigh. With him were Mrs. Di Jones of the South Herefordshire and Charlie Watts of the Cattistock who were to hunt hounds later that day.

"Tedworth Masters Bow Out" is the caption to a panoramic photograph showing excited horses streaming across the rough grasses of Salisbury Plain before a backdrop of thorn and scrub. A frieze of movement, the galloping horsemen are captured for a millisecond, like a clip from a film spectacular.

"Hey!" said a wag standing at the back of Westcourt stableyard. "We've been taken over!" And there was a general titter all round. Admittedly there appeared to be as many Royal Artillery subscribers as there were Tedworth at Rupert's Open Evening in summer 1993. They came to eye the refurbished kennels and wish him well. Peace after discord.

Captain Rupert Inglesant recently retired from the R.A. had no experience of hunting hounds. However his father was Secretary of the Quorn for eighteen successful seasons, so Rupert has followed the Quorn, Cottesmore and Fernie, and been able to watch the very best huntsmen, Captain Fanshawe, Michael Farrin and Bruce Durno. He has also whipped-in for five to six seasons to the Royal Artillery Foxhounds.

At the same time the Tedworth is most fortunate in having David Jukes as kennelhuntsman. Previously as amateur whipper-in to Captain Simon Clark of the South and West Wilts, he helped in kennels and in the country. A better grounding is hard to imagine. He then secured the position of first whipper-in to Martin Thornton at the Zetland, whom he succeeded as huntsman.

Hounds must be the first consideration. Rupert needed a pack with drive and fox sense to show sport and catch foxes. Thus drafts were obtained from fifteen different kennels including the Quorn, Zetland, Puckeridge, Avon Vale, New Forest and Blackmore and Sparkford Vale. Although hounds are not a level pack, with their experience, drive and cry they have accounted for thirty brace in their first season. A no mean achievement. Future breeding policy has to be dictated by hunting ability. At present no new stallion-blood is being sought outside the pack, but traditional lines such as the original "W" line are to be blended with more modern ones.

The most spectacular cub-hunting morning was on 7 October 1993 at Collingbourne, where forestry tracks are vibrant with Tedworth memories. The Honourable Mrs. Mirabel Helme was field Master that day, and living so close to the meet, she did not leave Mount Orleans until first light had coloured thin-crowned pines, which shelter the nineteenth century house from wind off Salisbury Plain.

Mount Orleans, like its counterpart across the valley Hougoumont Farm, are named, so they say, after Battle of Waterloo salients. A possible story, as the victorious Duke often hunted these woods. The spirits of the place say that Mount Orleans is a happy house of horses, hens and sheep. An Irish home. A house of children, set in a hide-and-seek garden; with mother's songs caught in a poet's rhyme.

That cub-hunting morning, her green velvet cap would have remained on its peg until the opening meet, meantime Mirabel's groom was tacking up horses in a square stable yard. Then together they passed through a blue metal gate, erected in quick-time one afternoon so combine harvesters could no longer break the peace of the courtyard.

Already at the meet in vehicles were the ever-present terrier team headed by Mr. Richard Whiteway, now joined by Mr. Richard Stokes. Also Mr. Sheppard with his wife, who farm their own land next to Heaven Corner and are wonderful rural neighbours of Mount Orleans, together with Mr. and Mrs. Stone. Miss Rhonda Small and Mrs. Gerry Beaton were the only mounted followers, and the Master sent Gerry off on her black horse to watch the vast expanse of Mr. Gordon's maize.

Hounds found in Heron's Copse. This fox had probably been on the move, and as Mirabel watched, hounds ran steadily past Heaven Corner with only the huntsman and David Jukes up. They flew on past Blackmore Lane before accounting for their quarry short of the open country on Wick Down. Stunned by the suddenness of this pipe-opener the field took a good ten minutes to catch up.

Following two more exciting woodland hunts on a plethora of foxes, hounds settled and got themselves together really well. Again the tempo was stepped up, and it was all followers could do to stay with them. Running the line once more through Cockshord hounds raced on to Cowcommon Bottom. Scent outside Joyce's Copse was poor. A weak line was carried across Sunton Heath before hounds marked by a small spinney, and their fox was accounted for.

Breakfast was at Mount Orleans where Mirabel's cooking is renowned, and guests might have recalled her book *Biddesden Cooking* and that she writes recipes for *Countryweek Hunting*. Trays of eggs stand on the hall table, and stone flags in the old house are cool during an Indian summer.

Sausages and eggs, brown eggs with rich yolks are served from pans. Gerry Beaton, her elbows on the table, claims to have had the hunt to herself for a fair portion of the time. She finds it difficult to remove the grin from her face long enough to eat - fortunate for David Jukes — who seizes the opportunity to consume the sausages!

"A splendid day," says Rupert. "A brace of foxes caught, and the vast majority of woodlands hunted through."

"No more than might be expected," observes Miss Small sharply, shaking white curls.

"Quite right! Quite Right!" The Master has to agree.

"Just think," and there is Australian mickey-taking in her tone. "Just imagine the risk the Hunt is taking, to have a new, untried Master."

"Rise above it!" says Mirabel "Rise above it!"

David Jukes chews the last sausage thoughtfully.

On 18 January 1994 her opinion was justified, when *Horse and Hound* came to report on Rhonda's meet at All Cannings, with approval. A large yellow kangaroo is painted on her garage door saying:

"Caution - Kangaroo for 25 kms!"

Pewsey Vale is notorious for roe deer and even the strange little muntjac, but kangaroo is unlikely. However, the pack sitting in an attentive, obedient bunch did not take adoring eyes off the Master, hot punch and sausage rolls being a sure indication of excitements to come.

Although it was a Tuesday, Tim Ormond was field Master, and of course, the Reads were there hunting their own farmland. John Jones as Secretary was taking caps, while John Milton, mounted, was there to enjoy the 'fruits' of his earth-stopping labours. How could we manage without John, Mr. Colin Almond and the whole of the Giddings family?

Hounds were taken to draw the set-aside by the canal bank, and to watch the fun, the faithful lined the roadside by open fields. Mr. Brian Sedgley, an amateur Tedworth whipper-in of long standing, who gave up riding only this year, is always there in his car. Charlie was soon away, and running the bank he went to ground at Allington swing-bridge.

Church Farm, Stanton, produced a fox for us in the best Read tradition, but was lost in Dogrun Covert under the curious White Horse, cut to watch the Vale in 1812. Another from the sticky-mud reeds of Mill Farm gave us a short burst. There are post and rail fences here, elegantly cleared by Lieutenant Colonel L. W. McNaught, formerly R.A., and organiser of their point-to-point. He is also a member of the Tedworth Hunt Committee. A further two of the field had paid the price in a bog.

"Go on. Go on," said a green collar. "Go on, or you'll lose them!"

Scent was difficult, and the fox was lost between canal and railroad. The *Horse and Hound* goes on:

"Hounds it seemed could run on turf but the moment they hit arable, which earlier had been frosted, they were brought up short. Again we had a brief burst with a fox from the First Covert hard by the railway, which allowed Rupert Inglesant to demonstrate an extremely clever cast forward to pick up his fox after two fields and soon after hounds marked to ground where he was left.

"It was tantalising. One sensed that, given a good fox, hounds would make us sit up and stare, but the scent was fickle and not to be trusted."

The afternoon grew cold. A strong dog fox bolted from Jim Read's straw barn, and Mrs. Kay Hastilow, as amateur whipper-in, galloped on for a view. He disappeared into a thick hedge, and hounds showed they had the scenting ability and drive to cast themselves as soon as they check.

Forcing him out, hound music echoed over the quiet hills, while their pilot flew through the Sands to Ford Wood. A series of jumps in the profusion of wire was exhilarating as Tim's chestnut showed the way, crossing the canal under Woodborough Hill.

The huntsman was unable to see where hounds last spoke. Patiently they worked out the line on the hard standing.

"Yoi!" a distant holloa from the canal brought the pack screaming across the arable, the note changing to a killing-cry. Surely the fox was beat. But in vain. The arable dissolved into a reed-pierced slime of bog-grass to defeat them.

In the pin-prick lights of Pewsey Vale farms and cottages, and "Looking Towards the Future", that good dog fox was given best.

The Tedworth look forward to hunting him another day.

Captain Rupert Inglesant, M.F.H., with hounds, hunting from All Cannings 1994. (Copyright Mr. Trevor Meeks.)

REFERENCES FOR CHAPTER 1. THROW YOUR HEART OVER

As detailed in the text, most of the source material for this chapter has been taken from "Reminiscences of the late Mr. Thomas Assheton Smith" by Sir John Eardley-Wilmot pub 1860.

1. "Costume of the Nineteenth Century" by C. W. Cunningham and Phillis Cunningham.
2. "A Hunting Pageant" by Mary Lovell, Saiga Books p 59.
3. "A History of Tidworth and Tedworth House" by David J. Croman, Phillimore.
4. As 1.
5. A reference to Lucy Glitters in Surtees' famous "Mr. Facey Romford's Hounds".
6. One of Mr. Smith's horses was named Fire King, as well as one of his yachts having the same name. Also ships called Fire Queen, Screw Queen, Glow-worm, Jenny Lind and Sea Serpent.
7. Dept. of Env. Lists of Buildings of Special arch. and hist. interest Dist. of Salisbury 1989.

8 & 9. As 3 p 16 et seq.

REFERENCES FOR CHAPTER 2. THE MARQUESS, THE PARSON AND TWO HUNTSMEN

1. "Reminiscences of the late Thomas Assheton Smith Esq", Chapter VIII by Sir John Eardley-Wilmot (Bart). John Murray 1860.

2 & 3. As 1 p 223.

4. George Carter 1792-1884 from "Hound and Horn".
5. "The Tedworth Hounds". Reprinted from "Salisbury and Winchester Journal" WHO-WHOOP.
6. As 1 p 287.

7 & 8. "The Wardens of Savernake Forest" by the Earl of Cardigan. Routledge and Paul p 300-306 London 1949.

9. As 1.

10, 11 & 12. "A History of Hunting in Hampshire", Brig.-Gen. J. F. R. Hope. Wykeham Press, Winchester.

13. Crockford Clerical Directory.
14. Information from Miss Sarah Fowle.
15. "Wiltshire Village Book", Michael Marsham. Pub. Countryside Books.
16. As 4.
17. As 14.

18 & 19. As 7.

20. As 10.
21. As 7.
22. As 4.

REFERENCES FOR CHAPTER 3. JACK'S THREE MASTERS AND THE RECTOR OF MILDENHALL

1. "Fox Hunting Recollections" by Sir Reginald Graham. Pub. 1908.
2. "A History of Hunting in Hampshire. The Tedworth Hunt" by Brig.-Gen. J. F. R. Hope. Pub. Warren & Co.
3. As 1.

4, 5 & 6. "A History of Tidworth and Tedworth House", David J. Croman. Pub. Phillimore.

7. "Forty Years of a Sportsman's Life", Sir Claude de Crespigny.
8. As 1.
9. As 4.
10. As 1.
11. Survey Map 1870. Sheet 77 Devizes. Pub. David & Charles.

12, 13, 14 & 15. As 1.

16. "Costume in the Nineteenth Century", C. W. and Phillis Cunningham.
17. As 1.
18. A Notice in the Savernake Forest Hotel. Francis Guise 1956.
19. "The Marlborough Times". "The Duke in Marlborough Country 1882".
20. As 2.
21. As 1.
22. "British Hunts and Huntsmen", 1904 edition.
23. "The Wardens of Savernake Forest", The Earl of Cardigan. Routledge and Paul, London 1949.
24. As 2.
25. "A History of Merrist Wood Agricultural College", 1945-82. Private pub. Printed by S.C.C. Supplies Dept.
26. "Short History up to 1908" from "Tales of the Tedworth". Pub. Tedworth Hunt.
27. As 2.
28. As 22.
29. As 26.

REFERENCES FOR CHAPTER 4. MR. YORKE SCARLETT AND THE ROYAL REGIMENT

1. "Minutes of the Salisbury Plain Committee". Appendix to Minute 419.

2
& 3. "Plain Soldiering", N. D. G. James. Hobnob Press.

4. Baily's Hunting Directory 1985-6.
5. Devizes (Salisbury Plain) OS map David & Charles, sheet 77 ISBN 071534442.
6. "Hare Hunting and Harriers", H. A. Bryden 1903.
7. "A History of Hunting in Hampshire", Brig.-Gen. J. F. R. Hope. Warren and Son p 288 et seq.

8, 9 & 10. Burke's Landed Gentry 1937.

11 & 12. "Gigha. The Flourishing Island", Kathleen Philip. Private pub. 1979.

13. "A History of Hunting in Hampshire", Brig. Gen. J. F. R. Hope, Warren & Son, Wykeham Press, Winchester.
14. "Hounds, Hares and Foxes of Larkhill", Estelle Holloway. Pub. R.A. Hunt 1992.
15. As 2 p 18.
16. As 13.
17. Ord. Survey map, Edward Stanford Ltd. Nineteenth century undated.
18. As 13.
19. As 11.
20. "The Tedworth Hunt. The Tedworth Woodland Hunt", W. Scarth Dixon. The Hunts Assn. 1926.
21. "Amesbury: Hist and des of". 2nd ed. Amesbury. Amesbury Soc 1989.
22. "A History of Tidworth and Tedworth House", David J. Croman. Phillimore p 38.

23 & 24. As 2 p 37 & 38.

25. As 17.
26. As 4.
27. As 2 p 95.
28. As 8.
29. As 11.
30. "British and Irish Hunts and Huntsmen", Volume III J. N. P. Watson. Batsford p 114.

REFERENCES FOR CHAPTER 5. SIR EDMUND ANTROBUS AND THE HUNT COMMITTEE

1. "Annual Report of School of Gunnery", 1912 Chief Instructor's letter.
2. "A Wiltshire Camera 1835-1914", David Burnett. Compton Russell. No 38.
3-7. "British Hunts and Huntsmen 1904", The Tedworth Hunt.
8 & 9. Inf. Sam Hart Esq., who lives at Shipton Bellinger and knows Charlie Perrin.
10 & 11. "Hunting in Hampshire", Brig.-Gen. J. F. R. Hope, Wykeham Press 1950.
12. Larousse "Modern Hist".
13 & 14. As 10.
15. As 10. Also report in the local paper (Heading removed).
16. As 12.
17. "With the Canadian Contingent". Pub. Can. Field Comforts Comm. 1915.

REFERENCES FOR CHAPTER 6. WAR AND PEACE

Most of the references for this chapter are taken from Hunt records.

1. "Army Airfield No. 2", "Netheravon". The Army Air Corps Journal No. 9 1983 p 34.
2. "A Wiltshire Camera", David Burnett. Compton Russell p 15.
3. Inf. Mr. H. C. Budden, Forest Manager, Wilts. & Avon Forest District.
4. Army List 1914. Batt RO, Mount Street, Taunton.
5. "Hounds, Hares and Foxes of Larkhill", Estelle Holloway. Pub. Royal Artillery Hunt, p 23.
6 & 7. "Hunting in Hampshire", Brig.-Gen. J. F. R. Hope. The Wykeham Press.
8. Burke's Landed Gentry 1937. Kingscote.
9. "A History of Tidworth and Tedworth House", David J. Croman. Phillimore.
10. "Modern History", Larousse, p 360.
11. "The Point-to-Point Calendar 1933". Hunting Diary and Guide.
12. Inf. supplied by Sam Hart Esq., joint author of "Shipton Bellinger". Private Pub.
13. "The Barrack Book 1929". 118 General 714, The War Office 1929.
14. As 9, p 51.
15. As 6.
16. Foxhound Kennel Studbook. Tedworth 1921 & 1922.
17. As 6.
18. As 9, p 48.

REFERENCES FOR CHAPTER 7. THE TEDWORTH WOODLAND FOXHOUNDS

1. Visit to Fyfield House by kind permission of G. B. Balding Esq.
2. Burke's "Peerage, Baronetage and Knightage" 1931.
3. As 2.
4. "The History of Savernake Forest" by the Marquess of Ailesbury.
5. Information from Brigadier Platt.
6. Information by Ruth Lady Dulverton.
7. As 5.
8. Local newspaper report. Heading removed.
9. Baily's "Hunting Directory".

REFERENCES FOR CHAPTER 8. SIR PETER FARQUHAR AND LORD MELCHETT

The author is indebted to Ruth Lady Dulverton and Mrs. Mary Saunders-Davies for their generous help and information for the source material in this chapter.

1, 2 & 3. Information from Ruth Lady Dulverton.

4 & 5. "British and Irish Hunts and Huntsmen", J. N. P. Watson. Batsford Vol. 1.

6 & 7. "The Book of the Foxhound", Daphne Moore. J. A. Allen, p 74.

8 & 9. Burke's "Peerage Baronetage and Knightage". 1931 edition.

10 & 11. Information from Mrs. Mary Saunders-Davies.

12. As 1.
13. As 6.
14. As 10.
15. Visit to Middlecot House by kind permission of Mr. and Mrs. C. L. Clarke.
16. "A History of Hunting in Hampshire" by Brig.-Gen. J. F. R. Hope. The Wykeham Press 1950.
17. Baily's Hunting Directory.

18 & 19. As 1.

20 & 21. "Hounds, Hares and Foxes of Larkhill", Estelle Holloway. Pub. Royal Artillery Hunt, p 51.

22. As 16.
23. Newspaper cutting source unknown.
24. As 10.
25. As 1.

REFERENCES FOR CHAPTER 9. SHADOWS THEN SUNSHINE

1. "Hunting in Hampshire", Brigadier-General J. F. R. Hope, Wykeham Press.

2 & 3. Burke's "Peerage, Barontage and Knightage", 1961.

4. Information Jim Read Esq.

5. "The History of Savernake Forest" by the Marquess of Ailesbury.

6. Information from the Countess of Cardigan.

7. "Hounds, Hares and Foxes of Larkhill", Estelle Holloway. R.A. Pub.

8. Visit to Rockley.

9 & 10. As 2.

APPENDIX FOR CHAPTER 2. THE MARQUESS, THE PARSON AND TWO HUNTSMEN

Field Masters 1858-79

Sir Edmund Antrobus (M.F.H. Old Surrey 1836-47) 1856-65, 2nd Baronet Antrobus', Co. Chester J.P., D.L., died 1870, also his two sons Edmund (afterwards Sir Edmund), M.P. East Surrey 1841-47, and Wilton, 1855-77, and Robert Crawford Antrobus, J.P. Middle and London.

Mr. W. Knatchbull arranged meets and draws resigned 1865.

Marquess of Ailesbury, field Master 1865-79.

Mr. F. Raikes of Netheravon, field Master.

Duke of Somerset, field Master.

Loaned country

New Forest Country, Sperry Well to Clarendon given up 1865.

APPENDIX FOR CHAPTER 5. SIR EDMUND ANTROBUS AND THE HUNT COMMITTEE

TEDWORTH HUNT COMMITTEES

WEST SIDE 1908-09	GENERAL COMMITTEE 1912
Marquess of Ailesbury (President)	Sir Edmund Antrobus (Chairman)
Sir Edmund Antrobus (Chairman)	H. G. Hornby
Hugh de Heinz Whatton	Dr. Stevens
F. Stratton	Colonel Harmar
G. Ferris	F. Sutton
Arthur Hussey (resigned 2 June, 1911)	Captain Malet
G. Young	Major Smith
H. Alexander	Colonel Boyle
G. McNiven (Secretary)	G. Young
Hon. Louis Greville, Heale House,	G. Ferris
Woodford, Salisbury	H. Alexander
G. P. Wilson	Wilton
Captain Popham, Master R.A.(B) Harriers	Hugh de H. Whatton
East End Manor Farm, Durrington	Admiral Marx
(resigned June 1912)	(Secretary)
Major Walford R.F.A. (replaced Popham)	E. McNiven

APPENDIX FOR CHAPTER 6. WAR AND PEACE 1915-1925

TEDWORTH HUNT COMMITTEE 1920-1921

EAST SIDE

G. B. Allen, Eastover, Andover

J. D. Best, Abbots Ann (Treasurer)
J. Dalton, Down Farm, Abbots Ann
Captain L. Edmunds, Cholderton (res.)

Captain Formby, Shipton Bellinger

W. H. Fowle, Chute Forest, Andover

Mrs. Hill, Redenham (died)

F. W. Lillywhite, Knights Enham, Andover
Admiral J. Marx, CB DSO, Clatford Lodge, Andover

F. R. Sutton, Penton Lodge, Andover
Major J. W. Smith, Weyhill
F. W. Yorke Scarlett, Fyfield
E. A. Wigan, Conholt Park, Andover
Lady Yarrow 14-5-24
Major Miller
Major Connop

WEST SIDE

Marquess of Ailesbury (Chairman)
H. Alexander, Upavon House
L. Arnold, West Chisenbury
G. Ferris, Milton Manor, Marlborough
Colonel E. Fowle, Charlton Manor
W. H. Gedding, Brimslade, Marlborough
R. Haynes, East Wick, Marlborough
E. McNiven, Manningford Abbotts (Secretary)
M. J. Read, Stanton St. Bernard
H. de Heinz Whatton, Rockley Manor, Marlborough

C. Young, Travancore, Pewsey
Lord Ernest St. Maur
Sir Leonard Powell 1923-24

1923-24 Colonel Cmmdt G. V. Horden
L. C. L. Oldfield
B. D. Fisher

Colonel B. D. F. Oldman

Garrison 1925-26
Sir William Heneker
Colonel Cmmdt. H. Stanley - Clarke
Colonel H. C. Jackson
Colonel Cmmdt. B. D. Fisher

APPENDIX FOR CHAPTER 9. SHADOWS THEN SUNSHINE

Part of:

Agreement between the Tedworth Hunt and the RA Hunt October 1951.

THE SCHEDULE

1. South of the Upavon-Urchfont road and west of the Upavon-Amesbury-Salisbury Road.

2. South and west of a line running . . . . . Alton . . . . . Ablington, thence along the Ablington . . . . . Bulford road, then east along Nine Mile River to Sheeps Bridge, thence following the Bulford . . . . . South Tidworth road to Long Barrows: there turning south-east to Althorne and thence along B 3084 until it strikes the main Stockbridge . . . . . Salisbury road, south of Nether Wallop.

APPENDIX FOR CHAPTER 11. RECOLLECTIONS!
OFFICERS OF THE TEDWORTH HUNT SUPPORTERS' CLUB

Chairman

1964-68	Group Captain Stansfeld
1968-72	F. Haskins
1972-78	J. Jones
1978-81	B. Read
1981-82	B. Read and R. Wheeler
1982-84	Mrs. S. Swanson
1984-89	J. Marshall
1989-	T. Hervey

Secretary

1964-68	H. Braun
1968-71	Miss J. Hibberd
1971-73	Mrs. J. Read
1973-77	Miss A. Bendall
1977-88	M. A. Robbins
1988-	Mrs. G. Beaton

Treasurer

1964-68	E. Green
1968-71	E. Andrews
1971-74	Mrs. Martin
1974-82	Miss R. Wakeford
1982-89	Mrs. C. Read
1989-91	Miss B. MacMullen
1991-	Mr. B. Tunmore